THE 100 CLUB

EVERY GOAL FROM ARSENAL'S GREATEST EVER SCORERS

NICK BROWN

First Edition.
First published 2022

Published by:
Morgan Lawrence Publishing Services Limited
16a Main Ridge West
Boston
Lincolnshire
PE21 6QQ
www.morganlawrence.co.uk
email: info@morganlawrence.co.uk
Company number: 12910264

(C) Nick Brown
ISBN: 9781838232955

A CIP catalogue record is available for this book from the British Library.

Photographs are courtesy of: Paul & Aline Burland CC BY-SA 2.0, Ronnie Macdonald, CC BY 2.0, joshjdss, CC BY 2.0, Ank kumar, CC BY-SA 4.0, Alexander Ottesen, CC BY-SA 2.5, Ed g2s, CC BY-SA 3.0, PA Images/Alamy Stock Photo, Speedpix/ Alamy Stock Photo.

Cover design by LC Graphix

Typesetting by Mathew Mann

Printed and bound in the United Kingdom

Contents

Introduction

Goals win games. It's an old football adage and it sounds blatantly obvious, but it is true. If you want to win football matches, you need someone who can find the back of the net. There is a reason why it tends to be the goal scorers who go for the biggest transfer fees.

For a player to score 100 goals for a club is a special thing. There have been 19 players in Arsenal's history to have reached that milestone, from Joe Baker who scored exactly 100, to Thierry Henry, the all time leading scorer with 228.

This book chronicles every goal scored by the members of Arsenal's 100 Club.

THE 100 CLUB

My goalscoring seemed to fall off a cliff after that match and I still regret that I didn't score more goals. I would have liked to score at least 150 for Arsenal, but I'm not going to moan.

When I look at the names of my fellow 100 club members, I'm humbled to be included amongst such illustrious company.

Happy reading!

Alan Smith
June 2022

THIERRY HENRY

Arsenal Goals:	*228*
Arsenal Debut:	*Arsenal v Leicester City, 7 August 1999*
First Arsenal Goal:	*Southampton v Arsenal, 18 September 1999*
Last Arsenal Goal:	*Sunderland v Arsenal, 11 February 2012*
Arsenal Honours:	*League Championship 2001/02, 2003/04*
	FA Cup 2002, 2003
	Charity / Community Shield 2002, 2004
Individual Honours:	*Golden Boot Winner 2001/02, 2003/04,*
	2004/05, 2005/06
	Europe Golden Shoe Winner 2003/04,
	2004/05
	PFA Player Of The Year 2002/03, 2003/04
	Football Writers Player Of The Year
	2002/03, 2003/04, 2005/06
	BBC Goal Of The Season 2003/04
	Knight Of The Legion Of Honour 1998
International Caps:	*123 (51 goals, France)*

Thierry Henry began his career at Monaco, under the tutelage of Arsène Wenger, capturing the Ligue 1 championship title in the 1996/97 season. He was part of the French squad that won the World Cup in 1998, although the main striking role was filled by Christophe Dugarry.

Henry joined Italian club Juventus in January 1999 but, playing as a wide man, struggled to make an impact and made the move to Arsenal in August of the same year for a reunion with Wenger. By his own admission he had to be "retaught everything about the art of striking" but when he got it, he certainly got it. He finished his first season in London with 26 goals and, in the summer, was a key figure as France won Euro 2000, scoring three goals in the tournament.

Returning to Arsenal after the Euros, Henry went from strength to strength. His partnership with Dennis Bergkamp was electric and in the 2001/02 season the Gunners finished seven points above second placed Liverpool to capture the Premier League title and defeated Chelsea 2-0 in the FA Cup final to claim the double. In 2003 he was runner-up in the FIFA World Player Of The Year awards to his countryman Zinedine Zidane who was playing for Real Madrid. In that 2002/03 season, he became the first player in history to score over 20 goals and make 20 assists in the same season in Europe's top five leagues – England, Italy, Spain, Germany and France.

The 2003/04 season saw Henry grab 39 goals in all competitions as Arsenal went the entire league season undefeated, a feat only ever done once before, back in the 1888/89 season by Preston North End. On 17 October 2005, Henry became Arsenal's all time leading scorer when he broke Ian Wright's previous record by scoring twice against Sparta Prague in the Champions League.

In June 2007, Henry joined Barcelona where he won two Spanish championships, two Copa Del Rey titles, two Champions Leagues, a UEFA Super Cup and the FIFA World Club Cup. He moved across the Pond to New York Red Bulls in 2010 and then, in January 2012, a loan deal brought him back to Arsenal. He picked up where he left off in the red and white, scoring on his debut and, in his last game, netting against Sunderland, his 228th and final Arsenal goal. He returned to Red Bulls after his loan period ended and announced his retirement in December 2014.

In 2008, he was voted the club's best ever player and, to mark the club's 125th anniversary, he was one of three players – the others being Dennis Bergkamp and Tony Adams – to have a statue erected outside the Emirates Stadium.

ARSENAL GOALS

Date	Opponents	Competition	Goals
18 September 1999	Southampton	League	1
22 September 1999	AIK Solna	Champions League	1
28 November 1999	Derby County	League	2
30 November 1999	Middlesbrough	League Cup	1
09 December 1999	Nantes	UEFA Cup	1
18 December 1999	Wimbledon	League	1
28 December 1999	Leeds United	League	1
15 January 2000	Sunderland	League	2
05 February 2000	Bradford City	League	1
02 March 2000	Deportivo La Coruña	UEFA Cup	2
09 March 2000	Deportivo La Coruña	UEFA Cup	1
16 March 2000	Werder Bremen	UEFA Cup	1
19 March 2000	Tottenham Hotspur	League	1
23 March 2000	Werder Bremen	UEFA Cup	1
26 March 2000	Coventry City	League	1
01 April 2000	Wimbledon	League	1
16 April 2000	Leeds United	League	1
20 April 2000	Lens	UEFA Cup	1
23 April 2000	Watford	League	2
06 May 2000	Chelsea	League	2
09 May 2000	Sheffield Wednesday	League	1
21 August 2000	Liverpool	League	1
26 August 2000	Charlton Athletic	League	2
06 September 2000	Chelsea	League	1
01 October 2000	Manchester United	League	1
14 October 2000	Aston Villa	League	1
28 October 2000	Manchester City	League	2
04 November 2000	Middlesbrough	League	1
05 December 2000	Bayern Munich	Champions League	1
09 December 2000	Newcastle United	League	1
26 December 2000	Leicester City	League	3
10 January 2001	Ipswich Town	League	1
13 January 2001	Lyon	Champions League	1
18 January 2001	Chelsea	FA Cup	1
25 February 2001	Manchester United	League	1

THE 100 CLUB

06 March 2001	Spartak Moscow	Champions League	1
31 March 2001	Tottenham Hotspur	League	1
04 April 2001	Valencia	Champions League	1
21 April 2001	Everton	League	1
18 August 2001	Middlesbrough	League	1
25 August 2001	Leicester City	League	1
08 September 2001	Chelsea	League	1
15 September 2001	Fulham	League	1
19 September 2001	Schalke	Champions League	2
29 September 2001	Derby County	League	2
13 October 2001	Southampton	League	1
16 October 2001	Panathinaikos	Champions League	2
20 October 2001	Blackburn Rovers	League	1
24 October 2001	Real Mallorca	Champions League	1
04 November 2001	Charlton Athletic	League	2
25 November 2001	Manchester United	League	2
01 December 2001	Ipswich Town	League	1
04 December 2001	Juventus	Champions League	1
09 December 2001	Aston Villa	League	2
23 December 2001	Liverpool	League	1
05 January 2002	Watford	FA Cup	1
23 January 2002	Leicester City	League	1
30 January 2002	Blackburn Rovers	League	1
23 February 2002	Fulham	League	2
27 February 2002	Beyer Leverkusen	Champions League	1
01 April 2002	Charlton Athletic	League	2
11 May 2002	Everton	League	2
18 August 2002	Birmingham City	League	1
24 August 2002	West Ham United	League	1
10 September 2002	Manchester City	League	1
14 September 2002	Charlton Athletic	League	1
21 September 2002	Bolton Wanderers	League	1
25 September 2002	PSV Eindhoven	Champions League	2
28 September 2002	Leeds United	League	1
30 October 2002	Borussia Dortmund	Champions League	1
16 November 2002	Tottenham Hotspur	League	1
27 November 2002	AS Roma	Champions League	3
30 November 2002	Aston Villa	League	2
26 December 2002	West Bromwich Albion	League	1

29 December 2002	Liverpool	League	1
01 January 2003	Chelsea	League	1
12 January 2003	Birmingham City	League	2
19 January 2003	West Ham United	League	3
09 February 2003	Newcastle United	League	1
22 February 2003	Manchester City	League	1
08 March 2003	Chelsea	FA Cup	1
19 March 2003	Valencia	Champions League	1
16 April 2003	Manchester United	League	2
19 April 2003	Middlesbrough	League	1
04 May 2003	Leeds United	League	1
11 May 2003	Sunderland	League	1
10 August 2003	Manchester United	Community Shield	1
16 August 2003	Everton	League	1
24 August 2003	Middlesbrough	League	1
27 August 2003	Aston Villa	League	1
13 September 2003	Portsmouth	League	1
26 September 2003	Newcastle United	League	2
18 October 2003	Chelsea	League	1
21 October 2003	Dynamo Kiev	Champions League	1
26 October 2003	Charlton Athletic	League	1
01 November 2003	Leeds United	League	2
25 November 2003	Inter Milan	Champions League	2
26 December 2003	Wolves	League	2
04 January 2004	Leeds United	FA Cup	1
10 January 2004	Middlesbrough	League	1
18 January 2004	Aston Villa	League	2
01 February 2004	Manchester City	League	1
07 February 2004	Wolves	League	1
10 February 2004	Southampton	League	2
28 February 2004	Charlton Athletic	League	1
06 March 2004	Portsmouth	FA Cup	2
10 March 2004	Celta Vigo	Champions League	2
13 March 2004	Blackburn Rovers	League	1
28 March 2004	Manchester United	League	1
09 April 2004	Liverpool	League	3
16 April 2004	Leeds United	League	4
15 May 2004	Leicester City	League	1
22 August 2004	Middlesbrough	League	2

THE 100 CLUB

25 August 2004	Blackburn Rovers	League	1
28 August 2004	Norwich City	League	1
18 September 2004	Bolton Wanderers	League	1
02 October 2004	Charlton Athletic	League	2
16 October 2004	Aston Villa	League	1
20 October 2004	Panathinaikos	Champions League	1
30 October 2004	Southampton	League	1
02 November 2004	Panathinaikos	Champions League	1
06 November 2004	Crystal Palace	League	1
13 November 2004	Tottenham Hotspur	League	1
24 November 2004	PSV Eindhoven	Champions League	1
04 December 2004	Birmingham City	League	2
07 December 2004	Rosenborg	Champions League	1
12 December 2004	Chelsea	League	2
26 December 2004	Fulham	League	1
05 February 2005	Aston Villa	League	1
14 February 2005	Crystal Palace	League	2
05 March 2005	Portsmouth	League	3
09 March 2005	Bayern Munich	Champions League	1
02 April 2005	Norwich City	League	3
14 August 2005	Newcastle United	League	1
24 August 2005	Fulham	League	2
18 September 2005	Sparta Prague	Champions League	2
02 October 2005	Sparta Prague	Champions League	1
05 October 2005	Sunderland	League	2
19 November 2005	Wigan Athletic	League	2
26 November 2005	Blackburn Rovers	League	1
28 December 2005	Portsmouth	League	2
14 January 2006	Middlesbrough	League	3
24 January 2006	Wigan Athletic	League Cup	1
01 February 2006	West Ham United	League	1
04 February 2006	Birmingham City	League	1
21 February 2006	Real Madrid	Champions League	1
04 March 2006	Fulham	League	2
12 March 2006	Liverpool	League	2
28 March 2006	Juventus	Champions League	1
01 April 2006	Aston Villa	League	2
12 April 2006	Portsmouth	League	1
22 April 2006	Tottenham Hotspur	League	1

01 May 2006	Sunderland	League	1
07 May 2006	Wigan Athletic	League	3
09 September 2006	Middlesbrough	League	1
23 September 2006	Sheffield United	League	1
26 September 2006	Porto	Champions League	1
14 October 2006	Watford	League	1
22 October 2006	Reading	League	2
18 November 2006	Newcastle United	League	1
02 January 2007	Charlton Athletic	League	1
06 January 2007	Liverpool	FA Cup	1
13 January 2007	Blackburn Rovers	League	1
21 January 2007	Manchester United	League	1
03 February 2007	Middlesbrough	League	1
09 January 2012	Leeds United	FA Cup	1
11 February 2012	Sunderland	League	1

IAN WRIGHT

Arsenal Goals: 185
Arsenal Debut: Leicester City v Arsenal, 25 September 1991
First Arsenal Goal: Leicester City v Arsenal, 25 September 1991
Last Arsenal Goal: West Ham United v Arsenal, 06 January 1998
Arsenal Honours: League Championship 1997/98
FA Cup 1993, 1998
European Cup Winners' Cup 1994
Individual Honours: Golden Boot Winner 1991/92
BBC Goal Of The Season 1989/90
MBE for services to football 2000
International Caps: 33 (9 goals, England)

Ian Wright came late into the professional game. Having played for Bermondsey based Sunday league club Ten-em-Be, he signed for non-league Greenwich Borough. After only a handful of games, he was invited to Crystal Palace for a trial and signed just before turning 22.

He established a lethal partnership with Mark Bright and Palace were promoted to the (old) first division. His first season in the top flight was ruined by injury but his comeback was as a substitute in the FA Cup final when he climbed off the bench to score twice in a 3-3 draw with Manchester United. Palace lost the replay 1-0.

George Graham brought him across London to Arsenal in September 1991 and his impact was immediate. A goal on his Gunners debut in the League Cup against Leicester was followed by a hat-trick on his league debut, a 4-0 win at Southampton. Wright was Arsenal's top scorer for six seasons in a row. In the 1992/93 season he was part of the Arsenal team that were the first team in history to win both domestic cup competitions in the same season, ironically beating Sheffield Wednesday in both League and FA Cup finals.

He was a key player in Arsène Wenger's first full season in charge, during which he became Arsenal's leading goal scorer of all time, eclipsing Cliff Bastin's club record. Wright's last goal at Highbury was the 300th of his career.

He moved to West Ham in 1998 and spent a season in East London before winding down his career with spells at Nottingham Forest, Celtic and Burnley. After retirement Wright became a media personality, not only as a football pundit, but in presenting tv and radio programmes.

ARSENAL GOALS

Date	Opponents	Competition	Goals
25 September 1991	Leicester City	League Cup	1
28 September 1991	Southampton	League	3
05 October 1991	Chelsea	League	1
08 October 1991	Leicester City	League Cup	1
26 October 1991	Notts County	League	1
16 November 1991	Oldham Athletic	League	1
01 December 1991	Tottenham Hotspur	League	1
12 December 1991	Everton	League	4
15 February 1992	Sheffield Wednesday	League	1
22 February 1992	Tottenham Hotspur	League	1
10 March 1992	Oldham Athletic	League	1
14 March 1992	West Ham United	League	2
28 March 1992	Wimbledon	League	1
08 April 1992	Norwich City	League	2
20 April 1992	Liverpool	League	2
02 May 1992	Southampton	League	3
23 August 1992	Liverpool	League	1
26 August 1992	Oldham Athletic	League	1
05 September 1992	Wimbledon	League	2
19 September 1992	Sheffield United	League	1
28 September 1992	Manchester City	League	1
03 October 1992	Chelsea	League	1
24 October 1992	Everton	League	1
02 November 1992	Crystal Palace	League	1
11 November 1992	Coventry City	League	1
01 December 1992	Derby County	League Cup	1
19 December 1992	Middlesbrough	League	1
02 January 1993	Yeovil Town	FA Cup	3
12 January 1993	Nottingham Forest	League Cup	2
03 February 1993	Leeds United	FA Cup	2
07 February 1993	Crystal Palace	League Cup	1
13 February 1993	Nottingham Forest	FA Cup	2
03 March 1993	Norwich City	League	1
06 March 1993	Ipswich Town	FA Cup	1
10 March 1993	Crystal Palace	League Cup	1

13 March 1993	Coventry City	League	1
21 April 1993	Nottingham Forest	League	1
08 May 1993	Crystal Palace	League	1
15 May 1993	Sheffield Wednesday	FA Cup	1
20 May 1993	Sheffield Wednesday	FA Cup	1
07 August 1993	Manchester United	Charity Shield	1
16 August 1993	Tottenham Hotspur	League	1
21 August 1993	Sheffield Wednesday	League	1
28 August 1993	Everton	League	2
11 September 1993	Ipswich Town	League	1
15 September 1993	Odense	Cup Winners Cup	1
21 September 1993	Huddersfield Town	League Cup	3
20 October 1993	Standard Liege	Cup Winners Cup	2
26 October 1993	Norwich City	League Cup	1
06 November 1993	Aston Villa	League	1
10 November 1993	Norwich City	League Cup	2
20 November 1993	Chelsea	League	1
27 November 1993	Newcastle United	League	1
06 December 1993	Tottenham Hotspur	League	1
12 December 1993	Sheffield Wednesday	League	1
27 December 1993	Swindon Town	League	1
29 December 1993	Sheffield United	League	1
01 January 1994	Wimbledon	League	1
22 January 1994	Oldham Athletic	League	1
31 January 1994	Bolton Wanderers	FA Cup	1
05 March 1994	Ipswich Town	League	3
19 March 1994	Southampton	League	3
29 March 1994	Paris St Germain	Cup Winners Cup	1
16 April 1994	Chelsea	League	1
23 April 1994	Aston Villa	League	2
20 August 1994	Manchester City	League	1
15 September 1994	Omonia Nicosia	Cup Winners Cup	1
18 September 1994	Newcastle United	League	1
21 September 1994	Hartlepool United	League Cup	2
25 September 1994	West Ham United	League	1
29 September 1994	Omonia Nicosia	Cup Winners Cup	2
01 October 1994	Crystal Palace	League	1
08 October 1994	Wimbledon	League	1
15 October 1994	Chelsea	League	2

20 October 1994	Brondby	Cup Winners Cup	1
23 October 1994	Coventry City	League	2
03 November 1994	Brondby	Cup Winners Cup	1
23 November 1994	Leicester City	League	1
30 November 1994	Sheffield Wednesday	League Cup	1
28 December 1994	Ipswich Town	League	1
14 January 1995	Everton	League	1
02 March 1995	Auxerre	Cup Winners Cup	1
16 March 1995	Auxerre	Cup Winners Cup	1
06 April 1995	Sampdoria	Cup Winners Cup	1
15 April 1995	Ipswich Town	League	3
17 April 1995	Aston Villa	League	2
20 April 1995	Sampdoria	Cup Winners Cup	1
29 April 1995	Tottenham Hotspur	League	1
20 August 1995	Middlesbrough	League	1
23 August 1995	Everton	League	1
10 September 1995	Manchester City	League	1
16 September 1995	West Ham United	League	1
19 September 1995	Hartlepool	League Cup	1
23 September 1995	Southampton	League	1
03 October 1995	Hartlepool	League Cup	3
14 October 1995	Leeds United	League	1
21 October 1995	Aston Villa	League	1
29 November 1995	Sheffield Wednesday	League Cup	1
23 December 1995	Liverpool	League	1
26 December 1995	Queens Park Rangers	League	1
30 December 1995	Wimbledon	League	1
06 January 1996	Sheffield United	FA Cup	1
10 January 1996	Newcastle United	League Cup	2
20 January 1996	Everton	League	1
23 March 1996	Newcastle United	League	1
06 April 1996	Leeds United	League	2
27 April 1996	Blackburn Rovers	League	1
24 August 1996	Leicester City	League	1
04 September 1996	Chelsea	League	1
10 September 1996	Mönchengladbach	UEFA Cup	1
16 September 1996	Sheffield Wednesday	League	3
21 September 1996	Middlesbrough	League	1
25 September 1996	Mönchengladbach	UEFA Cup	1

12 October 1996	Blackburn Rovers	League	2
23 October 1996	Stoke City	League Cup	1
26 October 1996	Leeds United	League	1
02 November 1966	Wimbledon	League	1
13 November 1996	Stoke City	League Cup	2
24 November 1996	Tottenham Hotspur	League	1
27 November 1996	Liverpool	League Cup	2
30 November 1996	Newcastle United	League	1
04 December 1996	Southampton	League	1
21 December 1996	Nottingham Forest	League	1
28 December 1996	Aston Villa	League	1
01 January 1997	Middlesbrough	League	1
29 January 1997	West Ham United	League	1
01 March 1997	Everton	League	1
24 March 1997	Liverpool	League	1
05 April 1997	Chelsea	League	1
21 April 1997	Coventry City	League	1
11 May 1997	Derby County	League	2
09 August 1997	Leeds United	League	1
11 August 1997	Coventry City	League	2
13 September 1997	Bolton Wanderers	League	3
24 September 1997	West Ham United	League	1
27 September 1997	Everton	League	1
04 October 1997	Barnsley	League	1
06 December 1997	Newcastle United	League	1
06 January 1998	West Ham United	League Cup	1

CLIFF BASTIN

Arsenal Goals:	*178*
Arsenal Debut:	*Arsenal v Everton, 5 October 1929*
First Arsenal Goal:	*Arsenal v Sheffield Wednesday, 4 January 1930*
Last Arsenal Goal:	*Arsenal v Blackburn Rovers, 30 August 1939*
Arsenal Honours:	*League Championship 1930/31, 1932/33, 1933/34, 1934/35, 1937/38*
	FA Cup 1930, 1936
	Charity / Community Shield 1930, 1931, 1933, 1934, 1938
Individual Honours:	*None*
International Caps:	*21 (12 goals, England)*

In the annals of Arsenal history, Cliff Bastin is up there with the very best. One of the mainstays of Arsenal's all-conquering team from the 1930s, Bastin was known for his deadly accuracy as well as his youthful looks that earned him the nickname 'Boy Bastin'.

His career began with Exeter City, his hometown club. He only played 17 matches for Exeter before making the move to Arsenal. Gunners' manager Herbert Chapman had gone to spy out a Watford player in a Watford v Exeter match but was so taken by Bastin's performance that he turned his attention to him instead.

He made his Arsenal debut at only 17 years of age and immediately became a first team regular. By the time he was 19, Bastin had won a league championship, an FA Cup and been capped by England. He is the youngest player in history to have achieved all three.

During his career at Highbury, Arsenal became the most famous club in the world due to Herbert Chapman's genius. His strategies and tactics were years before their time, with their opponents struggling to get to grips with his fast flowing counter-attacking style, with the emphasis being in individual skill and keeping possession. Bastin played a pivotal role in Chapman's masterplan. He was one of seven Arsenal players to be picked to play for England against the then world champions Italy in 1934, a record that still stands.

It is testament to Bastin that he is third in the list of Arsenal scorers, even though his career was interrupted for six years by the second world war. Had war not broken out, he most likely would have set scoring records that would never have been beaten.

ARSENAL GOALS

Date	Opponents	Competition	Goals
04 January 1930	Sheffield Wednesday	League	1
11 January 1930	Chelsea	FA Cup	1
18 January 1930	Burnley	League	1
25 January 1930	Birmingham City	FA Cup	1
15 February 1930	Middlesbrough	FA Cup	1
12 March 1930	Manchester United	League	1
22 March 1930	Hull City	FA Cup	1
12 April 1930	Sheffield United	League	1
19 April 1930	Huddersfield Town	League	1
21 April 1930	Leicester City	League	2
30 August 1930	Blackpool	League	2
10 September 1930	Blackburn Rovers	League	2
20 September 1930	Leicester City	League	1
27 September 1930	Birmingham City	League	1
11 October 1930	Derby County	League	1
25 October 1930	West Ham United	League	1
08 November 1930	Aston Villa	League	2
22 November 1930	Middlesbrough	League	2
25 December 1930	Manchester City	League	1
26 December 1930	Manchester City	League	1
27 December 1930	Blackpool	League	1
24 January 1931	Chelsea	FA Cup	1
28 January 1931	Grimsby Town	League	1
05 February 1931	Leicester City	League	2
14 February 1931	Derby County	League	3
21 February 1931	Manchester United	League	1
28 February 1931	West Ham United	League	1
11 March 1931	Leeds United	League	1
21 March 1931	Sheffield Wednesday	League	1
03 April 1931	Portsmouth	League	1
04 April 1931	Chelsea	League	1
18 April 1931	Liverpool	League	1
09 September 1931	Portsmouth	League	1
16 September 1931	Portsmouth	League	2
07 October 1931	West Bromwich Albion	Charity Shield	1

10 October 1931	Blackpool	League	3
05 December 1931	Sheffield Wednesday	League	1
19 December 1931	Middlesbrough	League	2
09 January 1932	Darwen	FA Cup	4
16 January 1932	Birmingham City	League	1
06 February 1932	Everton	League	1
13 February 1932	Portsmouth	FA Cup	1
17 February 1932	Grimsby Town	League	1
05 March 1932	Leicester City	League	1
12 March 1932	Manchester City	FA Cup	1
30 April 1932	Middlesbrough	League	2
03 September 1932	Sunderland	League	1
17 September 1932	Bolton Wanderers	League	1
01 October 1932	Blackpool	League	1
15 October 1932	Blackburn Rovers	League	1
22 October 1932	Liverpool	League	2
29 October 1932	Leicester City	League	2
05 November 1932	Wolves	League	2
19 November 1932	Aston Villa	League	1
03 December 1932	Portsmouth	League	2
10 December 1932	Chelsea	League	2
24 December 1932	Sheffield United	League	3
31 December 1932	Birmingham City	League	1
02 January 1933	Sheffield Wednesday	League	1
21 January 1933	Manchester City	League	2
01 February 1933	Bolton Wanderers	League	1
22 February 1933	Derby County	League	1
25 February 1933	Blackburn Rovers	League	2
08 April 1933	Middlesbrough	League	1
14 April 1933	Sheffield Wednesday	League	1
15 April 1933	Portsmouth	League	1
22 April 1933	Chelsea	League	2
29 April 1933	Huddersfield Town	League	2
02 September 1933	Sheffield Wednesday	League	1
06 September 1933	West Bromwich Albion	League	2
30 September 1933	Middlesbrough	League	1
07 October 1933	Blackburn Rovers	League	1
28 October 1933	Aston Villa	League	1
04 November 1933	Portsmouth	League	1

25 December 1933	Leeds United	League	1
27 January 1934	Crystal Palace	FA Cup	2
30 January 1934	Tottenham Hotspur	League	1
12 February 1934	Blackburn Rovers	League	1
24 March 1934	Wolves	League	1
31 March 1934	Stoke City	League	1
28 April 1934	Chelsea	League	1
25 August 1934	Portsmouth	League	1
01 September 1934	Liverpool	League	1
05 September 1934	Blackburn Rovers	League	1
15 September 1934	West Bromwich Albion	League	1
29 September 1934	Birmingham City	League	1
06 October 1934	Stoke City	League	2
13 October 1934	Manchester City	League	1
03 November 1934	Everton	League	2
17 November 1934	Aston Villa	League	1
28 November 1934	Manchester City	Charity Shield	1
15 December 1934	Leicester City	League	2
25 December 1934	Preston North End	League	1
19 January 1935	Leeds United	League	1
30 January 1935	West Bromwich Albion	League	1
02 February 1935	Sheffield Wednesday	League	1
16 February 1935	Reading	FA Cup	1
06 March 1935	Tottenham Hotspur	League	1
30 March 1935	Aston Villa	League	1
31 August 1935	Sunderland	League	1
21 September 1935	Manchester City	League	1
28 September 1935	Stoke City	League	2
05 October 1935	Blackburn Rovers	League	1
26 October 1935	Preston North End	League	1
16 November 1935	Everton	League	1
28 December 1935	Sunderland	League	1
11 January 1936	Bristol Rovers	FA Cup	2
19 February 1936	Newcastle United	FA Cup	2
29 February 1936	Barnsley	FA Cup	1
07 March 1936	Huddersfield Town	League	1
21 March 1936	Grimsby Town	FA Cup	1
11 April 1936	Middlesbrough	League	1
02 May 1936	Leeds United	League	1

12 September 1936	Sunderland	League	1
21 November 1936	Middlesbrough	League	1
23 January 1937	Wolves	League	1
30 January 1937	Manchester United	FA Cup	1
03 February 1937	Derby County	League	1
20 February 1937	Burnley	FA Cup	1
06 March 1937	West Bromwich Albion	FA Cup	1
13 March 1937	Leeds United	League	1
28 August 1937	Everton	League	1
01 September 1937	Huddersfield Town	League	1
04 September 1937	Wolves	League	1
20 November 1937	Charlton Athletic	League	1
27 November 1937	Leeds United	League	1
11 December 1937	Preston North End	League	1
25 December 1937	Blackpool	League	1
27 December 1937	Blackpool	League	1
08 January 1938	Bolton Wanderers	FA Cup	2
02 February 1938	Leicester City	League	1
12 March 1938	Middlesbrough	League	1
19 March 1938	Grimsby Town	League	2
23 April 1938	Preston North End	League	1
07 May 1938	Bolton Wanderers	League	2
05 November 1938	Leeds United	League	1
17 December 1938	Stoke City	League	1
07 January 1939	Chelsea	FA Cup	1
04 February 1939	Sunderland	League	1
30 August 1939	Blackburn Rovers	League	1

JOHN RADFORD

Arsenal Goals:	149
Arsenal Debut:	*West Ham United v Arsenal, 21 March 1964*
First Arsenal Goal:	*Arsenal v Wolves, 2 January 1965*
Last Arsenal Goal:	*Middlesbrough v Arsenal, 28 February 1976*
Arsenal Honours:	*League Championship 1970/71*
	FA Cup 1971
	Inter City Fairs / UEFA Cup 1970
Individual Honours:	*None*
International Caps:	*2 (0 goals, England)*

Radford came through the ranks at Arsenal before making his first team debut at West Ham in 1964, his only appearance of the 1963/64 season. The following season, though, saw him make his mark by becoming the club's youngest ever scorer of a hat-trick in a 4-1 win against Wolves at Highbury. At 17 years and 315 days, it is a record that still stands today. His first goal that day was also his first for the club.

For the 1966/67 season, Radford was a first team regular, having been moved from the centre out to the right wing by manager Bertie Mee. The 1968/69 season saw the start of Arsenal's reawakening. They hadn't won the league championship since 1952/53 and their last cup triumph had been in 1950, but under Mee's stewardship they reached the League Cup final, albeit they were on the end of a shock result as they were beaten by third division Swindon Town. Radford had by now been moved back into the centre of attack and was banging in the goals regularly.

The following season saw Arsenal end their trophy drought by winning the Inter City Fairs Cup, which would later be renamed the UEFA Cup and then the Europa League, by beating Anderlecht of Belgium 4-3 on aggregate in the two legged final.

Radford himself scored the second goal in Arsenal's 3-0 second leg victory.

The Inter City Cup win was a prelude to better things to come as in the following season, 1970/71, Arsenal secured their first league and cup double. Radford was central to their success, scoring 21 goals that season and forming a prolific partnership with Ray Kennedy. Even though he notched over 20 goals that campaign, Radford was more than just a scorer. It was from his assists that both of Arsenal's goals were scored in their 2-1 win over Liverpool in the FA Cup final.

Radford again had a big say in the FA Cup in the 1971/72 season, as he replaced injured goalkeeper Bob Wilson in the semi-final, keeping Stoke City at bay in a 1-1 draw. In the replay it was Radford's goal that took Arsenal to Wembley once more, although they were beaten in the final by Leeds.

Injury curtailed the latter part of his career for the Gunners and, unable to nail down a regular place, he moved across London to West Ham and then on to Blackburn Rovers. He ended his career in non-league football with Bishops Stortford, helping them to the Isthmian League title and the FA Trophy.

Radford has remained a fans' favourite and in recent times has been working for the club giving guided legends tours round the Emirates Stadium.

ARSENAL GOALS

Date	Opponents	Competition	Goals
02 January 1965	Wolves	League	3
09 January 1965	Darlington	FA Cup	1
16 January 1965	Sunderland	League	1
30 January 1965	Peterborough United	FA Cup	1
06 February 1965	Chelsea	League	1
20 February 1965	Fulham	League	1
23 February 1965	Tottenham Hotspur	League	1
25 September 1965	Manchester United	League	1
28 September 1965	Northampton Town	League	1
16 October 1965	Blackpool	League	1
11 December 1965	Liverpool	League	1
15 January 1966	Blackburn Rovers	League	1
29 January 1966	Stoke City	League	2
11 April 1966	West Bromwich Albion	League	1
23 August 1966	West Ham United	League	1
26 December 1966	Southampton	League	2
22 February 1967	Bolton Wanderers	FA Cup	3
06 May 1967	Stoke City	League	1
16 September 1967	Tottenham Hotspur	League	1
23 September 1967	Manchester City	League	1
14 October 1967	Sunderland	League	1
28 October 1967	Fulham	League	3
18 November 1967	Leicester City	League	1
05 December 1967	Burnley	League Cup	1
30 December 1967	Chelsea	League	1
17 January 1968	Huddersfield Town	League Cup	1
27 January 1968	Shrewsbury Town	FA Cup	1
09 March 1968	Birmingham City	FA Cup	1
30 April 1968	Sheffield Wednesday	League	1
04 May 1968	Sheffield Wednesday	League	1
10 August 1968	Tottenham Hotspur	League	1
17 August 1968	Liverpool	League	1
24 August 1968	Ipswich Town	League	1
27 August 1968	Manchester City	League	1
07 September 1968	Southampton	League	2

09 October 1968	Manchester City	League	1
12 October 1968	Coventry City	League	1
15 October 1968	Liverpool	League Cup	1
29 October 1968	Blackpool	League Cup	1
16 November 1968	Nottingham Forest	League	1
20 November 1968	Tottenham Hotspur	League Cup	1
04 December 1968	Tottenham Hotspur	League Cup	1
07 December 1968	Everton	League	1
26 December 1968	Manchester United	League	1
11 January 1969	Sheffield Wednesday	League	1
01 March 1969	Sheffield Wednesday	League	3
16 September 1969	Tottenham Hotspur	League	1
07 October 1969	West Bromwich Albion	League	1
01 November 1969	Crystal Palace	League	3
26 November 1969	Sporting de Portugal	Fairs Cup	1
06 December 1969	Southampton	League	1
13 December 1969	Burnley	League	1
03 January 1970	Blackpool	FA Cup	1
15 January 1970	Blackpool	FA Cup	1
14 February 1970	Everton	League	1
21 February 1970	Derby County	League	1
11 March 1970	Dinamo Bacau	Fairs Cup	1
14 March 1970	Liverpool	League	1
19 March 1970	Dinamo Bacau	Fairs Cup	2
30 March 1970	Crystal Palace	League	1
04 April 1970	West Ham United	League	1
28 April 1970	Anderlecht	Fairs Cup	1
22 August 1970	Manchester United	League	3
12 September 1970	Burnley	League	1
16 September 1970	Lazio	Fairs Cup	2
23 September 1970	Lazio	Fairs Cup	1
28 September 1970	Ipswich Town	League Cup	1
24 October 1970	Coventry City	League	1
31 October 1970	Derby County	League	1
07 November 1970	Blackpool	League	1
14 November 1970	Crystal Palace	League	1
28 November 1970	Liverpool	League	1
05 December 1970	Manchester City	League	1
12 December 1970	Wolves	League	1

06 January 1971	Yeovil Town	FA Cup	2
06 February 1971	Manchester City	League	1
20 February 1971	Ipswich Town	League	1
02 March 1971	Wolves	League	1
10 April 1971	Southampton	League	1
14 August 1971	Chelsea	League	1
25 September 1971	Leicester City	League	2
29 September 1971	Stromgodset	European Cup	2
06 October 1971	Newcastle United	League Cup	2
03 November 1971	Grasshoppers	European Cup	1
27 November 1971	Crystal Palace	League	1
11 December 1971	Coventry City	League	2
11 April 1972	Crystal Palace	League	1
19 April 1972	Stoke City	FA Cup	1
25 April 1972	Manchester United	League	1
15 August 1972	Wolves	League	2
23 September 1972	Norwich City	League	1
03 October 1972	Rotherham	League Cup	2
21 October 1972	Crystal Palace	League	1
31 October 1972	Sheffield United	League Cup	1
11 November 1972	Wolves	League	2
18 November 1972	Everton	League	1
02 December 1972	Leeds United	League	1
09 December 1972	Tottenham Hotspur	League	1
16 December 1972	West Bromwich Albion	League	1
26 December 1972	Norwich City	League	1
17 January 1973	Leicester City	FA Cup	1
10 February 1973	Liverpool	League	1
10 March 1973	Ipswich Town	League	1
23 April 1973	Southampton	League	1
28 April 1973	West Ham United	League	1
25 August 1973	Manchester United	League	1
22 September 1973	Stoke City	League	1
15 December 1973	Burnley	League	1
23 March 1974	Manchester City	League	2
13 April 1974	Chelsea	League	1
27 April 1974	Coventry City	League	1
24 August 1974	Manchester City	League	2
10 October 1974	Queens Park Rangers	League	1

16 October 1974	Manchester City	League	1
26 October 1974	West Ham United	League	1
11 January 1975	Carlisle United	League	1
19 February 1975	Leicester City	FA Cup	1
22 February 1975	Derby County	League	1
24 February 1975	Leicester City	FA Cup	1
20 December 1975	Burnley	League	1
24 February 1976	Liverpool	League	1
28 February 1976	Middlesbrough	League	1

JIMMY BRAIN

Arsenal Goals:	139
Arsenal Debut:	*Arsenal v Tottenham Hotspur, 25 October 1924*
First Arsenal Goal:	*Arsenal v Tottenham Hotspur, 25 October 1924*
Last Arsenal Goal:	*Arsenal v Manchester United, 21 February 1931*
Arsenal Honours:	*League Championship 1930/31 Charity / Community Shield 1930*
Individual Honours:	*None*
International Caps:	*None*

Welshman Jimmy Brain began his footballing career with local club Ton Pentre before getting his move to Arsenal. His career at Highbury could not have got off to a better start as he bagged a debut goal against local rivals Tottenham in October 1924.

The following season, 1925/26, saw him cement his name in Arsenal history as he became the first Gunner to score 30 league goals in a single season as he netted 34, as well as a further five in the FA Cup to end the season with 39. His tally remains second only to the 45 scored by Ted Drake in 1934/35.

Brain made an FA Cup final appearance in 1927, although the Gunners were famously beaten 1-0 by Cardiff City, the only time the cup has been won by a team outside of England. The following season saw him become the first player in Arsenal's history to hit 100 goals as he bagged a hat-trick against Liverpool in a 6-3 victory on 7 March 1928. He therefore became the founder member of the 100 Club.

Brain finally captured the championship medal his goal scoring feats deserved in 1930/31, ironically in his last season with the Gunners. At the end of that season, with his playing time in the previous couple of seasons having been limited thanks to the emergence of David Jack and Jack Lambert, who themselves would both become go on to score over 100 goals for the club, Brain moved across North London to Tottenham, the first player in history to cross the divide. He only stayed with Tottenham for a single season before moving on to Swansea Town and Bristol City. After retiring from playing, Brain held management positions at Kings Lynn and Cheltenham Town.

ARSENAL GOALS

Date	Opponents	Competition	Goals
25 October 1924	Tottenham Hotspur	League	1
01 November 1924	Bolton Wanderers	League	1
20 December 1924	Leeds United	League	4
21 January 1925	West Ham United	FA Cup	2
14 March 1925	Notts County	League	1
04 April 1925	Cardiff City	League	1
14 April 1925	West Bromwich Albion	League	1
18 April 1925	Burnley	League	3
31 August 1925	Leicester City	League	1
05 September 1925	Manchester United	League	1
07 September 1925	Leicester City	League	1
26 September 1925	Leeds United	League	2
05 October 1925	West Ham United	League	2
17 October 1925	Cardiff City	League	3
31 October 1925	Everton	League	3
07 November 1925	Manchester City	League	2
14 November 1925	Bury	League	3
21 November 1925	Blackburn Rovers	League	1
28 November 1925	Sunderland	League	1
09 January 1926	Wolves	FA Cup	1
16 January 1926	Manchester United	League	2
30 January 1926	Blackburn Rovers	FA Cup	1
06 February 1926	Leeds United	League	1
24 February 1926	Aston Villa	FA Cup	1
13 March 1926	Everton	League	3
17 March 1926	Sheffield United	League	2
27 March 1926	Bury	League	1
05 April 1926	Aston Villa	League	2
10 April 1926	Sunderland	League	1
01 May 1926	Birmingham City	League	2
06 September 1926	Bolton Wanderers	League	1
11 September 1926	Leicester City	League	1
15 September 1926	Manchester United	League	2
18 September 1926	Liverpool	League	1
16 October 1926	West Ham United	League	1

23 October 1926	Sheffield Wednesday	League	4
30 October 1926	Everton	League	1
06 November 1926	Blackburn Rovers	League	1
27 November 1926	West Bromwich Albion	League	1
04 December 1926	Bury	League	1
18 December 1926	Tottenham Hotspur	League	1
01 January 1927	Cardiff City	League	3
08 January 1927	Sheffield United	FA Cup	1
29 January 1927	Port Vale	FA Cup	1
10 February 1927	Leicester City	League	1
19 February 1927	Liverpool	FA Cup	1
26 February 1927	Burnley	League	4
12 March 1927	Sheffield Wednesday	League	1
15 April 1927	Aston Villa	League	2
16 April 1927	West Bromwich Albion	League	1
28 April 1927	Blackburn Rovers	League	1
30 April 1927	Birmingham City	League	1
07 May 1927	Tottenham Hotspur	League	2
27 August 1927	Bury	League	1
31 August 1927	Burnley	League	2
03 September 1927	Sheffield United	League	1
05 September 1927	Burnley	League	1
17 September 1927	Sunderland	League	1
01 October 1927	West Ham United	League	2
08 October 1927	Portsmouth	League	1
15 October 1927	Leicester City	League	1
03 December 1927	Huddersfield Town	League	1
10 December 1927	Newcastle United	League	1
27 December 1927	Liverpool	League	1
07 January 1928	Sheffield United	League	2
14 January 1928	West Bromwich Albion	FA Cup	1
28 January 1928	Everton	FA Cup	1
04 February 1928	Derby County	League	3
11 February 1928	West Ham United	League	2
18 February 1928	Aston Villa	FA Cup	2
07 March 1928	Liverpool	League	3
06 April 1928	Cardiff City	League	1
02 May 1928	Sheffield Wednesday	League	1
28 August 1928	Sheffield Wednesday	League	1

01 September 1928	Bolton Wanderers	League	1
22 September 1928	Manchester City	League	1
06 October 1928	Everton	League	1
20 October 1928	Newcastle United	League	1
27 October 1928	Liverpool	League	1
01 December 1928	Leicester City	League	1
08 December 1928	Manchester City	League	1
15 December 1928	Leeds United	League	1
22 December 1928	Burnley	League	1
25 December 1928	Blackburn Rovers	League	1
29 December 1928	Sheffield Wednesday	League	1
12 January 1929	Stoke City	FA Cup	1
19 January 1929	Portsmouth	League	1
20 February 1929	Swindon Town	FA Cup	1
23 February 1929	West Ham United	League	1
09 March 1929	Liverpool	League	1
16 March 1929	Cardiff City	League	1
29 March 1929	Blackburn Rovers	League	1
06 April 1929	Aston Villa	League	1
04 May 1929	Burnley	League	1
27 December 1930	Blackpool	League	3
21 February 1931	Manchester United	League	1

TED DRAKE

Arsenal Goals:	*139*
Arsenal Debut:	*Arsenal v Wolves, 24 March 1934*
First Arsenal Goal:	*Arsenal v Wolves, 24 March 1934*
Last Arsenal Goal:	*Arsenal v Brentford, 06 May 1939*
Arsenal Honours:	*League Championship 1934/35, 1937/38*
	FA Cup 1936
	Charity / Community Shield 1934, 1938
Individual Honours:	*None*
International Caps:	*5 (6 goals, England)*

Ted Drake's legacy in the game of football will forever be in place as the man who scored seven goals in a single league game, a record scoring feat in the top flight of English football. His amazing haul came on 14 December 1935 away at Aston Villa. He also had an eighth effort ruled out after it hit the crossbar and bounced down but not, according to the referee, over the line.

Drake began his career with his local club Southampton and, after just one full season, he came to Herbert Chapman's notice but turned down a move to Highbury to stay with the Saints. Two years later, with George Allison now Arsenal's manager, another move was made to recruit Drake and this time the transfer was concluded.

His Arsenal debut saw him score his first goal and, from then on, he never stopped. His first full season at Highbury, 1934/35, saw him bang in 44 goals, a club record that still stands today. He picked up a league championship medal, added an FA Cup the next season – it was Drake who scored the only goal of the game against Sheffield United – and another championship two seasons after that. He was one of the seven Arsenal players picked to play for England against Italy in 1934, scoring England's winner in a 3-2 victory.

The second world war interrupted Drake's goal getting escapades and, when the football programme resumed in peacetime, an injury picked up in a match against Reading in 1945 forced his retirement. After he stopped playing, he became manager of non-league Hendon before moving to Reading and onto Chelsea where he completely changed the culture of the club, introduced new training methods and was rewarded by leading them to their first league title in the 1954/55. Drake became the first person to win a league championship as both a player and manager.

Drake was quick, strong, powerful and deadly in front of goal, the perfect foil for Cliff Bastin who possessed dazzling skill. He was also an all round sportsman as, during his time with Southampton, he also played first class cricket with Hampshire.

ARSENAL GOALS

Date	Opponents	Competition	Goals
24 March 1934	Wolves	League	1
02 April 1934	Derby County	League	2
07 April 1934	Huddersfield Town	League	1
21 April 1934	Sunderland	League	1
05 May 1934	Sheffield United	League	2
25 August 1934	Portsmouth	League	1
01 September 1934	Liverpool	League	3
05 September 1934	Blackburn Rovers	League	2
08 September 1934	Leeds United	League	1
15 September 1934	West Bromwich Albion	League	1
24 September 1934	Birmingham City	League	4
20 October 1934	Tottenham Hotspur	League	3
27 October 1934	Sunderland	League	1
10 November 1934	Grimsby Town	League	1
24 November 1934	Chelsea	League	4
28 November 1934	Manchester City	Charity Shield	1
01 December 1934	Wolves	League	4
15 December 1934	Leicester City	League	3
29 December 1934	Portsmouth	League	1
05 January 1935	Liverpool	League	1
12 January 1935	Brighton	FA Cup	1
30 January 1935	West Bromwich Albion	League	1
06 March 1935	Tottenham Hotspur	League	2
16 March 1935	Everton	League	1
23 March 1935	Grimsby Town	League	1
30 March 1935	Aston Villa	League	1
06 April 1935	Chelsea	League	1
19 April 1935	Middlesbrough	League	4
22 April 1935	Middlesbrough	League	1
31 August 1935	Sunderland	League	2
07 September 1935	Birmingham City	League	1
11 September 1935	Grimsby Town	League	1
14 September 1935	Sheffield Wednesday	League	1
18 September 1935	Leeds United	League	1
26 October 1935	Preston North End	League	1

09 November 1935	Derby County	League	1
16 November 1935	Everton	League	1
23 November 1935	Wolves	League	2
14 December 1935	Aston Villa	League	7
28 December 1935	Sunderland	League	1
04 January 1936	Birmingham City	League	1
11 January 1936	Bristol Rovers	FA Cup	2
18 January 1936	Sheffield Wednesday	League	1
01 February 1936	Stoke City	League	1
18 April 1936	Aston Villa	League	1
25 April 1936	Sheffield United	FA Cup	1
27 April 1936	Chelsea	League	1
09 September 1936	Brentford	League	1
26 September 1936	Derby County	League	1
10 October 1936	Sheffield Wednesday	League	1
07 November 1936	Leeds United	League	1
14 November 1936	Birmingham City	League	2
21 November 1936	Middlesbrough	League	1
28 November 1936	West Bromwich Albion	League	2
05 December 1936	Manchester City	League	1
12 December 1936	Portsmouth	League	1
19 December 1936	Chelsea	League	1
25 December 1936	Preston North End	League	2
01 January 1937	Bolton Wanderers	League	4
16 January 1937	Chesterfield	FA Cup	2
23 January 1937	Wolves	League	1
30 January 1937	Manchester United	FA Cup	1
03 February 1937	Derby County	League	1
20 February 1937	Burnley	FA Cup	4
28 August 1937	Everton	League	3
01 September 1937	Huddersfield Town	League	1
04 September 1937	Wolves	League	2
11 September 1937	Leicester City	League	1
18 September 1937	Sunderland	League	1
20 November 1937	Charlton Athletic	League	1
27 November 1937	Leeds United	League	2
15 January 1938	Wolves	League	1
22 January 1938	Wolves	FA Cup	1
02 February 1938	Leicester City	League	1

16 February 1938	Manchester City	League	1
19 February 1938	Chelsea	League	1
05 March 1938	Stoke City	League	1
02 April 1938	Charlton Athletic	League	1
14 September 1938	Derby County	League	1
26 September 1938	Preston North End	Charity Shield	2
05 November 1938	Leeds United	League	1
12 November 1938	Liverpool	League	1
03 December 1938	Birmingham City	League	1
31 December 1938	Huddersfield Town	League	1
04 March 1939	Bolton Wanderers	League	2
11 March 1939	Leeds United	League	1
18 March 1939	Liverpool	League	1
25 March 1939	Leicester City	League	1
10 April 1939	Blackpool	League	1
15 April 1939	Manchester United	League	1
29 April 1939	Derby County	League	1
06 May 1939	Brentford	League	1

DOUG LISHMAN

Arsenal Goals:	*137*
Arsenal Debut:	*Sheffield United v Arsenal, 04 September 1948*
First Arsenal Goal:	*Arsenal v Tottenham Hotspur, 08 January 1949*
Last Arsenal Goal:	*Manchester United v Arsenal, 05 November 1955*
Arsenal Honours:	*League Championship 1952/53*
	Charity / Community Shield 1953
Individual Honours:	*None*
International Caps:	*None*

Doug Lishman's football career began with Walsall in 1946. He spent two seasons there before moving to Highbury in 1948. Remarkably, even though he is Arsenal's seventh top scorer of all time, his career with the Gunners was blighted by injury, including suffering a broken leg.

He joined Arsenal in 1948 and, having recovered from his injury problems, regained a regular place in the Gunners' line-up for the 1950/51 season. Arsenal reached the 1952 FA Cup final but were beaten 1-0 by Newcastle in a remarkable game that ended with the Gunners having only eight players on the pitch due to injuries, as there were no substitutes in those days.

The following season saw Arsenal finish as league champions, with Lishman providing the fire power. The goals continued to come in the next couple of seasons, but Lishman found his place in the side under threat during the 1955/56 campaign and, when the season ended, he transferred to Nottingham Forest in the second division. At Forest he scored a hat-trick against Sheffield United that gave them promotion to the first division, and Lishman retired from football in the summer of 1957.

ARSENAL GOALS

Date	Opponents	Competition	Goals
08 January 1949	Tottenham Hotspur	FA Cup	1
15 January 1949	Sheffield United	League	1
05 February 1949	Sunderland	League	1
05 March 1949	Burnley	League	1
02 April 1949	Birmingham City	League	1
09 April 1949	Middlesbrough	League	1
18 April 1949	Blackpool	League	2
27 April 1949	Manchester City	League	2
04 May 1949	Portsmouth	League	2
07 May 1949	Charlton Athletic	League	1
24 August 1949	Chelsea	League	1
03 September 1949	Liverpool	League	1
29 March 1950	Aston Villa	League	1
01 April 1950	Manchester City	League	1
10 April 1950	Stoke City	League	2
06 May 1950	Stoke City	League	3
02 September 1950	Sheffield Wednesday	League	1
09 September 1950	Middlesbrough	League	1
16 September 1950	Huddersfield Town	League	1
30 September 1950	West Bromwich Albion	League	2
14 October 1950	Manchester United	League	1
04 November 1950	Wolves	League	1
11 November 1950	Sunderland	League	4
18 November 1950	Liverpool	League	1
25 November 1950	Fulham	League	3
09 December 1950	Blackpool	League	1
21 April 1951	Bolton Wanderers	League	1
29 August 1951	Chelsea	League	1
01 September 1951	Sunderland	League	3
15 September 1951	Derby County	League	1
22 September 1951	Manchester City	League	1
27 October 1951	Fulham	League	3
03 November 1951	Middlesbrough	League	1
10 November 1951	West Bromwich Albion	League	3
24 November 1951	Bolton Wanderers	League	3

THE 100 CLUB

12 January 1952	Norwich City	FA Cup	2
26 January 1952	Manchester City	League	2
02 February 1952	Barnsley	FA Cup	1
23 February 1952	Leyton Orient	FA Cup	2
22 March 1952	Middlesbrough	League	1
07 April 1952	Chelsea	FA Cup	1
14 April 1952	Blackpool	League	2
19 April 1952	Stoke City	League	1
21 April 1952	West Bromwich Albion	League	1
23 August 1952	Aston Villa	League	1
30 August 1952	Sunderland	League	1
25 October 1952	Newcastle United	League	1
22 November 1952	Manchester City	League	1
20 December 1952	Aston Villa	League	1
03 January 1953	Sunderland	League	1
10 January 1953	Doncaster United	FA Cup	1
17 January 1953	Wolves	League	2
24 January 1953	Charlton Athletic	League	1
31 January 1953	Bury	FA Cup	1
07 February 1953	Tottenham Hotspur	League	1
14 February 1953	Burnley	FA Cup	1
18 February 1953	Derby County	League	2
14 March 1953	Newcastle United	League	2
04 April 1953	Liverpool	League	1
06 April 1953	Chelsea	League	1
15 April 1953	Bolton Wanderers	League	2
18 April 1953	Stoke City	League	3
01 May 1953	Burnley	League	1
12 September 1953	Sunderland	League	1
15 September 1953	Chelsea	League	2
19 September 1953	Manchester City	League	2
26 September 1953	Cardiff City	League	2
12 October 1953	Blackpool	Charity Shield	2
14 November 1953	Bolton Wanderers	League	1
21 November 1953	Liverpool	League	1
12 December 1953	West Bromwich Albion	League	2
19 December 1953	Huddersfield Town	League	1
26 December 1953	Blackpool	League	1
16 January 1954	Wolves	League	1

Date	Opponent	Competition	Goals
13 February 1954	Cardiff City	League	1
24 February 1954	Preston North End	League	1
13 March 1954	Charlton Athletic	League	1
24 April 1954	Middlesbrough	League	1
21 August 1954	Newcastle United	League	1
28 August 1954	West Bromwich Albion	League	1
31 August 1954	Everton	League	1
04 September 1954	Tottenham Hotspur	League	1
08 September 1954	Manchester City	League	1
11 September 1954	Sheffield United	League	1
14 September 1954	Manchester City	League	1
25 September 1954	Burnley	League	1
06 November 1954	Bolton Wanderers	League	1
13 November 1954	Huddersfield Town	League	1
01 January 1955	West Bromwich Albion	League	1
26 March 1955	Bolton Wanderers	League	2
09 April 1955	Blackpool	League	2
11 April 1955	Cardiff City	League	1
16 April 1955	Wolves	League	1
23 April 1955	Manchester United	League	2
17 September 1955	Portsmouth	League	1
24 September 1955	Sunderland	League	1
08 October 1955	Everton	League	1
29 October 1955	Charlton Athletic	League	1
05 November 1955	Manchester United	League	1

ROBIN VAN PERSIE

Arsenal Goals:	*132*
Arsenal Debut:	*Arsenal v Manchester United, 08 August 2004*
First Arsenal Goal:	*Manchester City v Arsenal, 27 October 2004*
Last Arsenal Goal:	*Arsenal v Norwich City, 05 May 2012*
Arsenal Honours:	*FA Cup 2005*
	Charity / Community Shield 2004
Individual Honours:	*Golden Boot Winner: 2011/12*
	PFA Player Of The Year 2011/12
	Football Writers Player Of The Year 2011/12
	BBC Goal Of The Season 2007/08
International Caps:	*102 (50 goals, Netherlands)*

Van Persie's career began at Feyenoord, for whom he made his debut at the age of 17. After three seasons, he left his native Netherlands to join Arsenal, who saw him as a long term successor to his compatriot Dennis Bergkamp.

Van Persie's Arsenal debut came in the 2004 Community Shield victory over Manchester United, and scored his first goal against their city rivals Manchester City in the League Cup that season. He was instrumental in helping Arsenal to win the 2005 FA Cup, coming on as a substitute and scoring in the penalty shoot-out victory over United. The following season, 2005/06, saw Arsenal reach the Champions League final, but Van Persie was an unused substitute as Barcelona carried off the trophy after a 2-1 victory.

After Thierry Henry joined Barcelona in the summer of 2007, Van Persie became Arsenal's main striker but, unfortunately, his career became a bit stop start due to injury problems. Despite this, he continued banging in the goals when he was available was selection.

ROBIN VAN PERSIE

The 2011/12 season saw Van Persie firing on all cylinders and he finished the season as Player Of The Year and Premier League top scorer with 30 goals. The season would be his last at the Emirates Stadium and he transferred to Manchester United in time for 2012/13.

Van Persie helped United to the Premier League title before moving to Turkey with Fenerbahçe and then heading home to the Netherlands to end his career where it started, at Feyenoord.

Not only was Van Persie a prolific goal scorer with his club teams, he also hit the heights internationally and is currently the Netherlands' leading scorer with 50 goals.

ARSENAL GOALS

Date	Opponents	Competition	Goals
27 October 2004	Manchester City	League Cup	1
30 October 2004	Southampton	League	1
07 December 2004	Rosenborg	Champions League	1
01 January 2005	Charlton Athletic	League	1
09 January 2005	Stoke City	FA Cup	1
19 March 2005	Blackburn Rovers	League	1
16 April 2005	Blackburn Rovers	FA Cup	2
02 May 2005	West Bromwich Albion	League	1
11 May 2005	Everton	League	1
14 August 2005	Newcastle United	League	1
25 October 2005	Sunderland	League Cup	2
02 November 2005	Sparta Prague	Champions League	2
05 November 2005	Sunderland	League	1
19 November 2005	Wigan Athletic	League	1
26 November 2005	Blackburn Rovers	League	1
29 November 2005	Reading	League Cup	1
24 January 2006	Wigan Athletic	League Cup	1
01 April 2006	Aston Villa	League	1
08 August 2006	Dinamo Zagreb	Champions League	1
30 September 2006	Charlton Athletic	League	2
22 October 2006	Reading	League	1
28 October 2006	Everton	League	1
21 November 2006	Hamburg	Champions League	1
29 November 2006	Fulham	League	1
23 December 2006	Blackburn Rovers	League	2
26 December 2006	Watford	League	1
02 January 2007	Charlton Athletic	League	2
21 January 2007	Manchester United	League	1
12 August 2007	Fulham	League	1
19 August 2007	Blackburn Rovers	League	1
19 September 2007	Sevilla	Champions League	1
29 September 2007	West Ham United	League	1
02 October 2007	Steaua Bucharest	Champions League	1
07 October 2007	Sunderland	League	2
29 March 2008	Bolton Wanderers	League	1
28 April 2008	Derby County	League	1

ROBIN VAN PERSIE

30 August 2008	Newcastle United	League	2
13 September 2008	Blackburn Rovers	League	1
30 September 2008	Porto	Champions League	2
18 October 2008	Everton	League	1
29 October 2008	Tottenham Hotspur	League	1
30 November 2008	Chelsea	League	2
21 December 2008	Liverpool	League	1
03 January 2009	Plymouth Argyle	FA Cup	2
28 January 2009	Everton	League	1
16 February 2009	Cardiff City	FA Cup	1
24 February 2009	AS Roma	Champions League	1
17 March 2009	Hull City	FA Cup	1
15 April 2009	Villarreal	Champions League	1
05 May 2009	Manchester United	Champions League	1
24 May 2009	Stoke City	League	2
12 September 2009	Manchester City	League	1
26 September 2009	Fulham	League	1
29 September 2009	Olympiakos	Champions League	1
04 October 2009	Blackburn Rovers	League	1
17 October 2009	Birmingham City	League	1
25 October 2009	West Ham United	League	1
31 October 2009	Tottenham Hotspur	League	2
03 May 2010	Blackburn Rovers	League	1
09 May 2010	Fulham	League	1
08 December 2010	Partizan Belgrade	Champions League	1
01 January 2011	Birmingham City	League	1
15 January 2011	West Ham United	League	2
19 January 2011	Leeds United	FA Cup	1
22 January 2011	Wigan Athletic	League	3
05 February 2011	Newcastle United	League	2
12 February 2011	Wolves	League	2
16 February 2011	Barcelona	Champions League	1
27 February 2011	Birmingham City	League Cup	1
19 March 2011	West Bromwich Albion	League	1
10 April 2011	Blackpool	League	1
17 April 2011	Liverpool	League	1
20 April 2011	Tottenham Hotspur	League	1
24 April 2011	Bolton Wanderers	League	1
08 May 2011	Stoke City	League	1

15 May 2011	Aston Villa	League	1
22 May 2011	Fulham	League	1
24 August 2011	Udinese	Champions League	1
28 August 2011	Manchester United	League	1
13 September 2011	Borussia Dortmund	Champions League	1
24 September 2011	Bolton Wanderers	League	2
16 October 2011	Sunderland	League	2
23 October 2011	Stoke City	League	2
29 October 2011	Chelsea	League	3
05 November 2011	West Bromwich Albion	League	1
19 November 2011	Norwich City	League	2
23 November 2011	Borussia Dortmund	Champions League	2
03 December 2011	Wigan Athletic	League	1
10 December 2011	Everton	League	1
21 December 2011	Aston Villa	League	1
31 December 2011	Queens Park Rangers	League	1
15 January 2012	Swansea	League	1
22 January 2012	Manchester United	League	1
29 January 2012	Aston Villa	FA Cup	2
04 February 2012	Blackburn Rovers	League	3
26 February 2012	Tottenham Hotspur	League	1
03 March 2012	Liverpool	League	2
06 March 2012	Inter Milan	Champions League	1
12 March 2012	Newcastle United	League	1
11 April 2012	Wolves	League	1
28 April 2012	Stoke City	League	1
05 May 2012	Norwich City	League	2

Jimmy Brain became the first player
to score 100 goals for Arsenal.

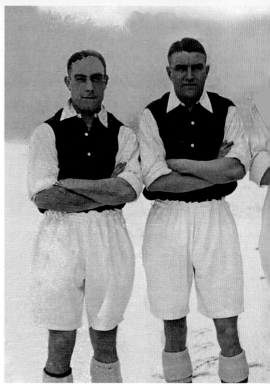

Cliff Bastin (left) and Ted Drake (right) scored
over 300 Arsenal goals between them.

Highbury was Arsenal's home for 93 years.

Ian Wright scored 185 times for Arsenal, including this goal in the 1993 FA Cup Final.

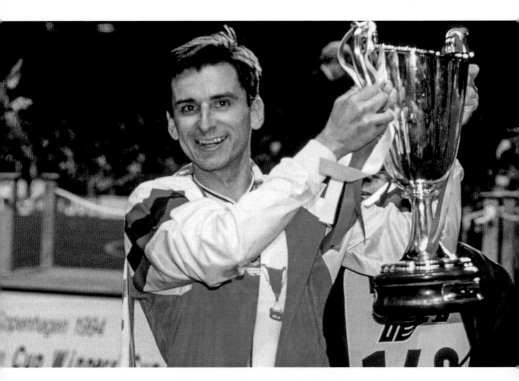

Alan Smith scored the only goal of the game as Arsenal
won the European Cup Winners' Cup Final in 1994.

Dutch international Dennis Bergkamp joined Arsenal for £7,500,000 in 1995.

Goals win games. They also win trophies.

Arsenal moved into the Emirates Stadium in 2006.

Robin Van Persie won the
FA Cup in 2005.

Theo Walcott became England's
youngest international in 2006.

Olivier Giroud became the latest member of 'the 100 club'
when he scored his 100th Arsenal goal in 2017.

Thierry Henry scored an incredible 228 goals for the Gunners.
Simply the greatest ever Arsenal goal scorer.

JOE HULME

Arsenal Goals:	*125*
Arsenal Debut:	*Leeds United v Arsenal, 06 February 1926*
First Arsenal Goal:	*Bury v Arsenal, 27 March 1926*
Last Arsenal Goal:	*Arsenal v Sunderland, 18 September 1937*
Arsenal Honours:	*League Championship 1930/31, 1932/33, 1934/35*
	FA Cup 1930, 1936
	Charity / Community Shield 1930, 1931
Individual Honours:	*None*
International Caps:	*9 (4 goals, England)*

A stalwart from the era of the legendary Herbert Chapman, Joe Hulme started off in non-league football with York City in the Midland League before joining Blackburn Rovers. After two years in Blackburn, he moved down to London in 1926, becoming one of Chapman's first major signings.

His impact was instant. He played his first game against Leeds United in February 1926, was chosen for a Football League XI and made his England international debut the following season against Scotland. He also played in the infamous 1927 FA Cup final when Arsenal were beaten 1-0 by Cardiff City.

Hulme was an Arsenal regular for the next few seasons, his pace making him a valuable asset in Chapman's game plan. With Hulme on one side and Cliff Bastin on the other side, supported by Alex James in the midfield, Arsenal were dangerous opponents for anyone they came up against. They won the FA Cup in 1930 and the league championship in both the 1930/31 and 1932/33 seasons.

Arsenal retained the title in 1933/34, although injury problems robbed Hulme of a prominent role that season. He was only able to manager eight appearances, not enough to earn a medal, but still scored five goals in those games. He did, however, feature more regularly the following year as Arsenal completed a hat-trick of title triumphs, although his injury problems were beginning to take their toll. The 1935/36 season saw him win another FA Cup medal as the Gunners beat Sheffield United. He is the only player to have played in Arsenal's first four FA Cup finals, in 1927, 1930, 1932 and 1936.

Hulme's last Arsenal appearance was against Liverpool in 1937 and left for Huddersfield in 1938, for whom he only made eight appearances before retiring from playing.

Hulme was also a first class cricketer, representing Middlesex on 225 occasions as a middle order batter and medium pace bowler. Arsenal have a rich history of footballer / cricketers. Joining Hulme on the list are Andy Ducat (Surrey), Wally Hardinge (Kent), Arthur Milton (Gloucester), Denis Compton (Middlesex), Leslie Compton (Middlesex), Ted Drake (Hampshire), Don Roper (Hampshire), Jim Standen (Worcestershire), Ray Swallow (Derbyshire), Joe North (Middlesex), Henry White (Warwickshire) and Sir Harry Storer (Derbyshire).

ARSENAL GOALS

Date	Opponents	Competition	Goals
27 March 1926	Bury	League	1
17 April 1926	Huddersfield Town	League	1
01 September 1926	Bolton Wanderers	League	2
06 September 1926	Bolton Wanderers	League	1
11 September 1926	Leicester City	League	1
27 November 1926	West Bromwich Albion	League	1
08 January 1927	Sheffield United	FA Cup	1
26 March 1927	Southampton	FA Cup	1
28 April 1927	Blackburn Rovers	League	1
04 May 1927	Bury	League	2
03 September 1927	Sheffield United	League	1
08 October 1927	Portsmouth	League	1
12 November 1927	Middlesbrough	League	1
10 December 1927	Newcastle United	League	1
24 December 1927	Everton	League	1
14 January 1928	West Bromwich Albion	FA Cup	1
28 January 1928	Everton	FA Cup	2
18 February 1928	Aston Villa	FA Cup	1
07 March 1928	Liverpool	League	1
06 April 1928	Cardiff City	League	1
18 April 1928	Middlesbrough	League	1
10 November 1928	Sheffield United	League	1
22 December 1928	Burnley	League	1
29 December 1928	Sheffield Wednesday	League	1
12 January 1929	Stoke City	FA Cup	1
23 February 1929	West Ham United	League	1
09 March 1929	Liverpool	League	2
31 August 1929	Leeds United	League	1
07 September 1929	Sheffield Wednesday	League	1
14 September 1929	Burnley	League	1
05 October 1929	Everton	League	1
19 October 1929	Grimsby Town	League	1
09 November 1929	Birmingham City	League	2
14 December 1929	Huddersfield Town	League	1
26 December 1929	Portsmouth	League	1

12 March 1930	Manchester United	League	1
29 March 1930	Blackburn Rovers	League	1
09 April 1930	Middlesbrough	League	1
12 April 1930	Sheffield United	League	1
19 April 1930	Huddersfield Town	League	1
01 September 1930	Bolton Wanderers	League	1
13 September 1930	Sunderland	League	1
15 September 1930	Blackburn Rovers	League	1
20 September 1930	Leicester City	League	1
08 October 1930	Sheffield Wednesday	Charity Shield	1
25 December 1930	Manchester City	League	1
26 December 1930	Manchester City	League	1
14 January 1931	Aston Villa	FA Cup	2
28 January 1931	Grimsby Town	League	1
05 February 1931	Leicester City	League	1
07 February 1931	Sheffield United	League	1
14 February 1931	Derby County	League	1
21 February 1931	Manchester United	League	1
04 April 1931	Chelsea	League	1
25 April 1931	Newcastle United	League	2
31 August 1931	Blackburn Rovers	League	1
05 September 1931	Birmingham City	League	1
12 September 1931	Sunderland	League	2
26 September 1931	Everton	League	1
10 October 1931	Blackpool	League	1
17 October 1931	Bolton Wanderers	League	1
14 November 1931	West Ham United	League	1
28 November 1931	Liverpool	League	1
25 December 1931	Sheffield United	League	1
09 January 1932	Darwen	FA Cup	2
16 January 1932	Birmingham City	League	1
23 January 1932	Plymouth Argyle	FA Cup	1
06 February 1932	Everton	League	1
13 February 1932	Portsmouth	FA Cup	1
05 March 1932	Leicester City	League	1
19 March 1932	Newcastle United	League	1
03 September 1932	Sunderland	League	3
17 September 1932	Bolton Wanderers	League	1
08 October 1932	Derby County	League	1

29 October 1932	Leicester City	League	3
12 November 1932	Newcastle United	League	1
26 November 1932	Middlesbrough	League	1
10 December 1932	Chelsea	League	1
26 December 1932	Leeds United	League	1
25 February 1933	Blackburn Rovers	League	2
25 March 1933	Newcastle United	League	1
08 April 1933	Middlesbrough	League	3
14 April 1933	Sheffield Wednesday	League	2
18 November 1933	Stoke City	League	1
02 December 1933	Liverpool	League	1
10 March 1934	Aston Villa	League	1
14 April 1934	Liverpool	League	2
10 November 1934	Grimsby Town	League	1
24 November 1934	Chelsea	League	1
15 December 1934	Leicester City	League	3
25 December 1934	Preston North End	League	2
12 January 1935	Brighton	FA Cup	1
26 January 1935	Leicester City	FA Cup	1
30 January 1935	West Bromwich Albion	League	1
23 November 1935	Wolves	League	1
25 December 1935	Liverpool	League	1
26 December 1935	Liverpool	League	1
25 January 1936	Liverpool	FA Cup	1
15 February 1936	Newcastle United	FA Cup	1
25 March 1936	Everton	League	1
10 April 1936	West Bromwich Albion	League	1
29 April 1936	Bolton Wanderers	League	1
04 September 1937	Wolves	League	1
18 September 1937	Sunderland	League	1

DAVID JACK

Arsenal Goals: *124*
Arsenal Debut: *Arsenal v Newcastle United, 20 October 1928*
First Arsenal Goal: *Arsenal v Sheffield United, 10 November 1928*
Last Arsenal Goal: *Arsenal v Aston Villa, 10 March 1934*
Arsenal Honours: *League Championship 1930/31, 1932/33, 1933/34*
     FA Cup 1930
     Charity / Community Shield 1930, 1931, 1933
Individual Honours: *None*
International Caps: *9 (3 goals, England)*

Born in Lancashire, David Jack was the son of Scottish footballer Bob Jack who had played for Alloa Athletic before moving south. He started his career at one of his father's former clubs, Plymouth Argyle, before moving back to Bolton, the town of his birth for what was a world record transfer fee of £3,500. He spent eight seasons at Bolton where he scored the first ever goal at Wembley Stadium, the winner in a 1-0 FA Cup final victory over West Ham.

In 1928, Herbert Chapman took advantage of Bolton's perilous financial situation and swooped for Jack, paying the Trotters at least £10,000 for his services (some sources say as much as £11,500). This was another world record transfer fee. Legend has it that Chapman met the Bolton directors in a hotel bar, ordered his own gin and tonics with no gin in them but asked the bartender to serve doubles to the Bolton officials. He thus managed to knock the price down considerably to what he thought was reasonable. At the time of writing, only three other players in history have twice moved in world record deals – the first was Alf Common who moved from Sheffield United to Sunderland and then Sunderland to Middlesbrough, then came Jack, then Diego Maradona who moved from Boca Juniors to Barcelona and then on to Napoli, and finally the Brazilian Ronaldo in his moves between PSV Eindhoven to Barcelona and Barcelona to Inter Milan.

At Arsenal, Jack was an instant success and his partnership with Jack Lambert was one of the most prolific ever seen. He was in the team that won the FA Cup in 1930 and captured a hat-trick of league championships in the 1930/31, 1932/33 and 1933/34 seasons. He retired after the third title success and had a brief stint in management with Sheffield United, Middlesbrough and Shelbourne.

Testament to how good a footballer David Jack was is that he twice moved between clubs for a world record fee, he is not only amongst Arsenal's greatest ever goal scorers but he is also still Bolton's third highest scorer as well, he was the first player to win the FA Cup at Wembley with two different clubs and, as of 2022, he is one of only three men who have scored over 100 league goals for two different English top flight teams along with Jimmy Greaves and Alan Shearer.

ARSENAL GOALS

Date	Opponents	Competition	Goals
10 November 1928	Sheffield United	League	1
24 November 1928	Aston Villa	League	2
08 December 1928	Manchester United	League	2
25 December 1928	Blackburn Rovers	League	1
05 January 1929	Bolton Wanderers	League	2
19 January 1929	Portsmouth	League	2
26 January 1929	Mansfield Town	FA Cup	1
09 February 1929	Huddersfield Town	League	1
23 February 1929	West Ham United	League	1
13 March 1929	Birmingham City	League	1
16 March 1929	Cardiff City	League	1
23 March 1929	Sheffield United	League	1
30 March 1929	Bury	League	4
02 April 1929	Newcastle United	League	1
06 April 1929	Aston Villa	League	1
20 April 1929	Manchester United	League	1
22 April 1929	Everton	League	1
04 May 1929	Burnley	League	2
31 August 1929	Leeds United	League	2
04 September 1929	Manchester City	League	1
07 September 1929	Sheffield Wednesday	League	1
11 September 1929	Manchester City	League	2
14 September 1929	Burnley	League	1
09 November 1929	Birmingham City	League	1
27 November 1929	Middlesbrough	League	1
14 December 1929	Huddersfield Town	League	1
18 January 1930	Burnley	League	1
25 January 1930	Birmingham City	FA Cup	1
08 March 1930	West Ham United	League	2
22 March 1930	Hull City	FA Cup	1
26 March 1930	Hull City	FA Cup	1
30 August 1930	Blackpool	League	2
06 September 1930	Leeds United	League	1
08 October 1930	Sheffield Wednesday	Charity Shield	1
01 November 1930	Huddersfield Town	League	1

DAVID JACK

Date	Opponent	Competition	Goals
08 November 1930	Aston Villa	League	2
29 November 1930	Chelsea	League	3
13 December 1930	Liverpool	League	1
20 December 1930	Newcastle United	League	1
25 December 1930	Manchester City	League	1
27 December 1930	Blackpool	League	3
10 January 1931	Aston Villa	FA Cup	1
14 January 1931	Aston Villa	FA Cup	1
28 January 1931	Grimsby Town	League	4
05 February 1931	Leicester City	League	1
14 February 1931	Derby County	League	1
21 February 1931	Manchester United	League	1
28 February 1931	West Ham United	League	2
14 March 1931	Aston Villa	League	1
21 March 1931	Sheffield Wednesday	League	1
28 March 1931	Middlesbrough	League	2
18 April 1931	Liverpool	League	1
02 May 1931	Bolton Wanderers	League	2
19 September 1931	Manchester City	League	2
26 September 1931	Everton	League	1
24 October 1931	Leicester City	League	1
31 October 1931	Aston Villa	League	1
07 November 1931	Newcastle United	League	1
14 November 1931	West Ham United	League	3
21 November 1931	Chelsea	League	1
28 November 1931	Liverpool	League	2
05 December 1931	Sheffield Wednesday	League	2
12 December 1931	Huddersfield Town	League	1
19 December 1931	Middlesbrough	League	2
09 January 1932	Darwen	FA Cup	3
17 February 1932	Grimsby Town	League	1
20 February 1932	Blackpool	League	1
28 March 1932	Derby County	League	1
16 April 1932	Sheffield Wednesday	League	1
03 September 1932	Sunderland	League	1
10 September 1932	Manchester City	League	1
14 September 1932	West Bromwich Albion	League	1
24 September 1932	Everton	League	1
15 October 1932	Blackburn Rovers	League	1

29 October 1932	Leicester City	League	1
05 November 1932	Wolves	League	3
19 November 1932	Aston Villa	League	1
26 November 1932	Middlesbrough	League	1
03 December 1932	Portsmouth	League	1
24 December 1932	Sheffield United	League	1
31 December 1932	Birmingham City	League	1
02 January 1933	Sheffield Wednesday	League	1
22 February 1933	Derby County	League	1
01 April 1933	Aston Villa	League	1
22 April 1933	Chelsea	League	1
26 August 1933	Birmingham City	League	1
02 September 1934	Sheffield Wednesday	League	1
30 September 1934	Middlesbrough	League	2
17 February 1934	Derby County	FA Cup	1
10 March 1934	Aston Villa	League	1

DENNIS BERGKAMP

Arsenal Goals: 120
Arsenal Debut: *Arsenal v Middlesbrough, 20 August 1995*
First Arsenal Goal: *Arsenal v Southampton, 23 September 1995*
Last Arsenal Goal: *West Bromwich Albion v Arsenal, 15 April 2006*
Arsenal Honours: *League Championship 1997/98, 2001/02, 2003/04*
FA Cup 1998, 2002, 2003, 2005
Charity / Community Shield 1998, 2002, 2004
Individual Honours: *PFA Player Of The Year 1997/98*
Football Writers Player Of The Year 1997/98
BBC Goal Of The Season 1997/98, 2001/02
International Caps: *79 (37 goals, Netherlands)*

Dennis Bergkamp began his career at Ajax where he was a product of their youth academy, with Johan Cruyff giving him his professional debut in 1986. He went on to win an Eredivisie league title, two KNVB Cup winner's medals, a European Cup Winners' Cup and UEFA Cup with the Amsterdam club.

In 1993, along with his Ajax team-mate Wim Jonk, Bergkamp moved to Italy with Inter Milan, gaining his second UEFA Cup medal in his first season there. In 1995, Milan were purchased by Italian businessman Massimo Moratti who promised to make big changes after their disappointing 1993/94 season, Bergkamp's second with the club. One such change saw him sanction the Dutchman's transfer to Arsenal in June 1995.

The move to Highbury reignited Bergkamp's career and, over the course of the next eleven years, he became to be regarded as one of the finest players of his generation and his partnership with

Thierry Henry one of the most feared in world football. He played a pivotal role in Arsenal's success under the stewardship of Arsène Wenger, the most successful in the club's history. At Arsenal, Bergkamp won three Premier League titles and four FA Cups. The 2003/04 season saw Bergkamp play a major role in Arsenal going the entire league season unbeaten, a feat never seen before in the Premier League and only once before in English football history, by Preston North End in the league's inaugural season in 1888/89.

Fittingly, his last goal for Arsenal came on 'Dennis Bergkamp Day', on 15 April 2006. It was Arsenal's last season at Highbury Stadium before their move to the Emirates Stadium, and also Bergkamp's last season before retirement. He was given a special day with the whole stadium decked out in Dutch orange for him. The first game at the new stadium also focussed on Bergkamp, as he was given a testimonial against Ajax.

Bergkamp epitomised the beautiful football played by Wenger's Arsenal. He was skilful and graceful but also had the killer instinct. His goal against Newcastle in the 2001/02 season was voted the best ever Premier League goal in the league's 25th anniversary celebrations in 2017. He is also the only player in history to have been voted in first, second and third place in the *Match Of The Day* 'Goal Of The Month' competition, a feat he achieved in August 1997.

One final honour for Bergkamp came in 2011 when he was one of three players, along with Thierry Henry and Tony Adams, to have statues unveiled of them at Arsenal's stadium as part of the club's 125th anniversary celebrations.

ARSENAL GOALS

Date	Opponents	Competition	Goals
23 September 1995	Southampton	League	2
03 October 1995	Hartlepool United	League Cup	2
14 October 1995	Leeds United	League	1
24 October 1995	Barnsley	League Cup	1
04 November 1995	Manchester United	League	1
18 November 1995	Tottenham Hotspur	League	1
21 November 1995	Sheffield Wednesday	League	1
03 February 1996	Coventry City	League	1
10 February 1996	Nottingham Forest	League	1
14 February 1996	Aston Villa	League Cup	2
02 March 1996	Queens Park Rangers	League	1
16 March 1996	Wimbledon	League	1
05 May 1996	Bolton Wanderers	League	1
17 August 1996	West Ham United	League	1
24 August 1996	Leicester City	League	1
26 October 1996	Leeds United	League	1
13 November 1996	Stoke City	League Cup	1
24 November 1996	Tottenham Hotspur	League	1
01 January 1997	Middlesbrough	League	1
15 January 1997	Sunderland	FA Cup	1
19 January 1997	Everton	League	1
19 February 1997	Manchester United	League	1
01 March 1997	Everton	League	1
08 March 1997	Nottingham Forest	League	2
05 April 1997	Chelsea	League	1
11 May 1997	Derby County	League	1
23 August 1997	Southampton	League	2
27 August 1997	Leicester City	League	3
21 September 1997	Chelsea	League	2
24 September 1997	West Ham United	League	1
30 September 1997	PAOK Salonika	UEFA Cup	1
04 October 1997	Barnsley	League	2
18 November 1997	Coventry City	League Cup	1
04 January 1998	Port Vale	FA Cup	1
17 January 1998	Coventry City	League	1

31 January 1998	Southampton	League	1
18 February 1998	Chelsea	League Cup	1
25 February 1998	Crystal Palace	FA Cup	1
08 March 1998	West Ham United	FA Cup	1
28 March 1998	Sheffield Wednesday	League	1
13 April 1998	Blackburn Rovers	League	1
18 April 1998	Wimbledon	League	1
25 April 1998	Barnsley	League	1
04 October 1998	Newcastle United	League	2
21 October 1998	Dynamo Kiev	Champions League	1
13 December 1998	Aston Villa	League	2
20 December 1998	Leeds United	League	1
24 January 1999	Wolves	FA Cup	1
31 January 1999	Chelsea	League	1
06 February 1999	West Ham United	League	1
23 February 1999	Sheffield United	FA Cup	1
09 March 1999	Sheffield Wednesday	League	2
13 March 1999	Everton	League	1
06 April 1999	Blackburn Rovers	League	1
14 April 1999	Manchester United	FA Cup	1
29 April 1999	Wimbledon	League	1
07 August 1999	Leicester City	League	1
10 August 1999	Derby County	League	1
19 October 1999	Barcelona	Champions League	1
20 November 1999	Middlesbrough	League	2
25 November 1999	Nantes	UEFA Cup	1
26 February 2000	Southampton	League	1
02 March 2000	Deportivo La Coruña	UEFA Cup	1
12 March 2000	Middlesbrough	League	1
06 April 2000	Lens	UEFA Cup	1
23 September 2000	Ipswich Town	League	1
28 October 2000	Manchester City	League	1
27 January 2001	Queens Park Rangers	FA Cup	1
03 February 2001	Coventry City	League	1
21 February 2001	Lyon	Champions League	1
18 August 2001	Middlesbrough	League	2
15 September 2001	Fulham	League	1
20 October 2001	Blackburn Rovers	League	1
24 October 2001	Real Mallorca	Champions League	1

05 January 2002	Watford	FA Cup	1
27 January 2002	Liverpool	FA Cup	1
30 January 2002	Blackburn Rovers	League	2
27 February 2002	Bayer Leverkusen	Champions League	1
02 March 2002	Newcastle United	League	1
23 March 2002	Newcastle United	FA Cup	1
30 March 2002	Sunderland	League	1
11 May 2002	Everton	League	1
17 September 2002	Borussia Dortmund	Champions League	1
23 November 2002	Southampton	League	1
04 January 2003	Oxford United	FA Cup	1
25 January 2003	Farnborough Town	FA Cup	1
29 January 2003	Liverpool	League	1
22 February 2003	Manchester City	League	1
04 May 2003	Leeds United	League	1
22 November 2003	Birmingham City	League	1
14 December 2003	Blackburn Rovers	League	1
24 January 2004	Middlesbrough	FA Cup	1
07 February 2004	Wolves	League	1
20 March 2004	Bolton Wanderers	League	1
15 August 2004	Everton	League	1
22 August 2004	Middlesbrough	League	1
28 August 2004	Norwich City	League	1
23 January 2005	Newcastle United	League	1
01 February 2005	Manchester United	League	1
15 February 2005	Crystal Palace	League	1
11 May 2005	Everton	League	1
15 May 2005	Birmingham City	League	1
14 September 2005	Thun	Champions League	1
28 December 2005	Portsmouth	League	1
15 April 2006	West Bromwich Albion	League	1

REG LEWIS

Arsenal Goals:	*118*
Arsenal Debut:	*Arsenal v Everton, 01 January 1938*
First Arsenal Goal:	*Arsenal v Everton, 01 January 1938*
Last Arsenal Goal:	*Leyton Orient v Arsenal, 23 February 1952*
Arsenal Honours:	*League Championship 1947/48*
	FA Cup 1950
	Charity / Community Shield 1948
Individual Honours:	*None*
International Caps:	*2 (2 goals, England)*

Reg Lewis was a one club man. He was born in Staffordshire but spent his entire career at Highbury after having been raised in London. He scored on his league debut against Everton on New Year's Day 1938 but missed out on a league championship medal that season due to only making four appearances.

He made inroads into gaining a regular first team place the following season but the outbreak of war in 1939 brought his progress to a halt. After hostilities ended in 1945, Lewis became a regular and Arsenal's main goal threat. The 1947/48 season saw him get his hands on that elusive championship medal and he scored both goals in the Gunners' 2-0 victory over Liverpool in the FA Cup final of 1950.

Unfortunately for Lewis, injuries began to curtail his career and he was forced into retirement in 1953.

ARSENAL GOALS

Date	Opponents	Competition	Goals
01 January 1938	Everton	League	1
05 February 1938	Derby County	League	1
17 December 1938	Stoke City	League	2
21 January 1939	Charlton Athletic	League	1
28 January 1939	Aston Villa	League	2
04 February 1939	Sunderland	League	1
25 February 1939	Preston North End	League	1
31 August 1946	Wolves	League	1
04 September 1946	Blackburn Rovers	League	1
07 September 1946	Sunderland	League	2
11 September 1946	Everton	League	2
14 September 1946	Aston Villa	League	1
17 September 1946	Blackburn Rovers	League	2
28 September 1946	Manchester United	League	1
12 October 1946	Brentford	League	1
26 October 1946	Chelsea	League	1
02 November 1946	Sheffield United	League	1
16 December 1946	Leeds United	League	2
23 December 1946	Liverpool	League	1
30 December 1946	Bolton Wanderers	League	1
04 January 1947	Sunderland	League	2
15 March 1947	Preston North End	League	3
22 March 1947	Leeds United	League	1
05 April 1947	Bolton Wanderers	League	1
26 April 1947	Grimsby Town	League	4
31 May 1947	Everton	League	1
27 August 1947	Charlton Athletic	League	1
03 September 1947	Charlton Athletic	League	4
06 September 1947	Manchester United	League	1
27 September 1947	Burnley	League	1
25 October 1947	Everton	League	1
27 December 1947	Liverpool	League	1
01 January 1948	Bolton Wanderers	League	1
03 January 1948	Sheffield United	League	1
17 January 1948	Manchester United	League	1

31 January 1948	Preston North End	League	2
15 September 1948	Liverpool	League	1
25 September 1948	Wolves	League	2
06 September 1948	Manchester United	Charity Shield	2
09 September 1948	Burnley	League	2
06 November 1948	Birmingham City	League	1
13 November 1948	Middlesbrough	League	1
27 November 1948	Portsmouth	League	1
11 December 1948	Charlton Athletic	League	1
27 December 1948	Derby County	League	1
05 February 1949	Sunderland	League	1
19 February 1949	Wolves	League	2
26 February 1949	Bolton Wanderers	League	1
19 March 1949	Newcastle United	League	1
15 April 1949	Blackpool	League	1
07 September 1949	West Bromwich Albion	League	1
10 September 1949	Huddersfield	League	1
14 September 1949	West Bromwich Albion	League	1
17 September 1949	Bolton Wanderers	League	1
24 September 1949	Birmingham City	League	1
01 October 1949	Derby County	League	2
08 October 1949	Everton	League	2
22 October 1949	Blackpool	League	1
19 November 1949	Charlton Athletic	League	1
26 November 1949	Aston Villa	League	1
24 December 1949	Sunderland	League	1
07 January 1950	Sheffield Wednesday	FA Cup	1
14 January 1950	Huddersfield	League	1
21 January 1950	Bolton Wanderers	League	1
11 February 1950	Burnley	FA Cup	1
04 March 1950	Leeds United	FA Cup	1
01 April 1950	Manchester City	League	2
15 April 1950	Newcastle United	League	1
29 April 1950	Liverpool	FA Cup	2
06 May 1950	Stoke City	League	1
11 January 1951	Carlisle United	FA Cup	2
13 January 1951	Middlesbrough	League	2
20 January 1951	Huddersfield Town	League	2
27 January 1951	Northampton Town	FA Cup	2

10 March 1951	Derby County	League	2
17 March 1951	Aston Villa	League	1
14 April 1951	Fulham	League	1
13 October 1951	Burnley	League	1
01 December 1951	Stoke City	League	1
15 December 1951	Huddersfield Town	League	1
22 December 1951	Wolves	League	2
25 December 1951	Portsmouth	League	1
02 February 1952	Barnsley	FA Cup	3
16 February 1952	Preston North End	League	2
23 February 1952	Leyton Orient	FA Cup	1

ALAN SMITH

Arsenal Goals:	*115*
Arsenal Debut:	*Arsenal v Liverpool, 15 August 1987*
First Arsenal Goal:	*Arsenal v Portsmouth, 29 August 1987*
Last Arsenal Goal:	*Manchester City v Arsenal, 12 December 1994*
Arsenal Honours:	*League Championship 1988/89, 1990/91*
	FA Cup 1993
	League Cup 1993
	Charity / Community Shield 1991
	European Cup Winners' Cup 1994
Individual Honours:	*Golden Boot Winner 1988/89, 1990/91*
International Caps:	*13 (2 goals, England)*

Alan Smith began his career playing non-league football with Alvechurch in 1981 and was snapped up by Leicester City the following year. In the 1982/83 season he struck up a prolific partnership with Gary Lineker as Leicester won promotion to the First Division. The Lineker / Smith spearhead was a successful one and it wasn't long before both moved on, Lineker first to Everton in 1985 and Smith to Arsenal in 1987. He was loaned back to the Foxes for the rest of that season and became a full-time Gunner for the start of the 1987/88 season.

A classic old-fashioned number nine, Smith was an excellent target man. He was deadly in the air, had a surprisingly good touch for a big centre-forward and could hold the ball up brilliantly whilst waiting for others to bring into play.

His first Arsenal goal came at Highbury against Portsmouth in 1987, and he became a key figure as manager George Graham rebuilt the Gunners at returned them to the top of the English game. That season they were beaten in the League Cup final, although Smith netted one of Arsenal's goals in the 3-2 loss against Luton Town.

As the winners' medals began to come, not only was Smith a scorer or many goals, he was also a scorer of important goals. He headed the first in Arsenal's famous 2-0 victory over Liverpool at Anfield in 1989 which secured the Gunners their first league championship title since 1970/71, and he also scored the only goal of the game in the European Cup Winners' Cup final against Parma of Italy in 1994. Between the two he picked up another championship medal in 1990/91 and both League Cup and FA Cup medals in the 1992/93 season as Arsenal became the first team to win both domestic cup competitions in the same season.

He was forced to retire in the summer 1995 at the age of 32 due to a knee injury. After his playing days, Smith joined the media and became a regular co-commentator on Sky Sports.

ARSENAL GOALS

Date	Opponents	Competition	Goals
29 August 1987	Portsmouth	League	3
12 September 1987	Nottingham Forest	League	1
19 September 1987	Wimbledon	League	1
23 September 1987	Doncaster Rovers	League Cup	1
27 October 1987	Bournemouth	League Cup	1
31 October 1987	Newcastle United	League	1
01 January 1988	Portsmouth	League	1
20 February 1988	Manchester United	FA Cup	1
24 February 1988	Everton	League Cup	1
27 February 1988	Charlton Athletic	League	1
06 March 1988	Tottenham Hotspur	League	1
04 April 1988	Norwich City	League	1
24 April 1988	Luton Town	League Cup	1
30 April 1988	Sheffield Wednesday	League	1
27 August 1988	Wimbledon	League	3
03 September 1988	Aston Villa	League	1
10 September 1988	Tottenham Hotspur	League	1
17 September 1988	Southampton	League	1
24 September 1988	Sheffield Wednesday	League	1
01 October 1988	West Ham United	League	2
12 October 1988	Hull City	League Cup	2
22 October 1988	Queens Park Rangers	League	1
25 October 1988	Luton Town	League	1
06 November 1988	Nottingham Forest	League	1
04 December 1988	Liverpool	League	1
31 December 1988	Aston Villa	League	1
14 January 1989	Everton	League	1
04 February 1989	West Ham United	League	1
11 February 1989	Millwall	League	1
25 February 1989	Luton Town	League	1
11 March 1989	Nottingham Forest	League	1
01 May 1989	Norwich City	League	2
13 May 1989	Derby County	League	1
26 May 1989	Liverpool	League	1
09 September 1989	Sheffield Wednesday	League	1

19 September 1989	Plymouth Argyle	League Cup	1
03 October 1989	Plymouth Argyle	League Cup	1
25 October 1989	Liverpool	League Cup	1
28 October 1989	Derby County	League	1
18 November 1989	Queens Park Rangers	League	1
26 November 1989	Liverpool	League	1
16 December 1989	Luton Town	League	1
01 January 1990	Crystal Palace	League	2
31 March 1990	Everton	League	1
05 May 1990	Norwich City	League	2
25 August 1990	Wimbledon	League	1
09 October 1990	Chester City	League Cup	1
17 November 1990	Southampton	League	2
24 November 1990	Queens Park Rangers	League	1
28 November 1990	Manchester United	League Cup	2
02 December 1990	Liverpool	League	1
08 December 1990	Luton Town	League	1
26 December 1990	Derby County	League	2
29 December 1990	Sheffield United	League	2
01 January 1991	Manchester City	League	1
05 January 1991	Sunderland	FA Cup	1
02 February 1991	Chelsea	League	1
23 February 1991	Crystal Palace	League	1
30 March 1991	Derby County	League	2
03 April 1991	Aston Villa	League	2
06 April 1991	Sheffield United	League	1
14 April 1991	Tottenham Hotspur	FA Cup	1
06 May 1991	Manchester United	League	3
11 May 1991	Coventry City	League	1
24 August 1991	Aston Villa	League	1
27 August 1991	Luton Town	League	1
31 August 1991	Manchester City	League	1
03 September 1991	Leeds United	League	2
14 September 1991	Crystal Palace	League	1
18 September 1991	Austria Memphis	European Cup	4
21 September 1991	Sheffield United	League	1
26 October 1991	Notts County	League	1
08 December 1991	Nottingham Forest	League	1
04 January 1992	Wrexham	FA Cup	1

08 February 1992	Notts County	League	1
15 February 1992	Sheffield Wednesday	League	1
02 May 1992	Southampton	League	1
17 October 1992	Nottingham Forest	League	1
07 November 1992	Coventry City	League	1
03 February 1993	Leeds United	FA Cup	1
07 February 1993	Crystal Palace	League Cup	2
10 April 1993	Ipswich Town	League	1
05 October 1993	Huddersfield Town	League Cup	1
03 November 1993	Standard Liege	Cup Winners Cup	1
20 November 1993	Chelsea	League	1
27 November 1993	Newcastle United	League	1
09 February 1994	Bolton Wanderers	FA Cup	1
02 April 1994	Swindon Town	League	1
04 May 1994	Parma	Cup Winners Cup	1
21 September 1994	Hartlepool United	League Cup	1
08 October 1994	Wimbledon	League	1
20 October 1994	Brondby	Cup Winners Cup	1
12 December 1994	Manchester City	League	1

JACK LAMBERT

Arsenal Goals:	*109*
Arsenal Debut:	*Arsenal v Bolton Wanderers, 06 September 1926*
First Arsenal Goal:	*Arsenal v West Ham United, 16 October 1926*
Last Arsenal Goal:	*Arsenal v West Bromwich Albion, 06 September 1933*
Arsenal Honours:	*League Championship 1930/31, 1932/33 FA Cup 1930 Charity / Community Shield 1930, 1931*
Individual Honours:	*None*
International Caps:	*None*

Jack Lambert was a big strong centre forward whose career began in strange circumstances. He was born in Yorkshire and signed by Leeds in 1922 and, without having played a single game, he was poached by Rotherham and made his debut the following year, scoring the only goal of the game against Bradford City. The Football Association saw Rotherham's move as illegal and ordered Lambert back to Leeds, fining Rotherham heavily. He played a single game back at Leeds before moving to Doncaster Rovers in a swap deal involving goalkeeper David Russell.

He made his mark at Doncaster and was noticed by Herbert Chapman, then manager of Huddersfield Town. After moving to Arsenal, Chapman signed Lambert in 1926. For the first couple of years, Lambert was in and out of the team, but he became a regular during the 1929/30 season. Lambert scored in the FA Cup final that year, a 2-0 victory over Chapman's old team Huddersfield.

The 1930/31 season saw Lambert knocking in 38 goals in just 34 matches, including his notching seven hat-tricks, a club record for a single season that he shares with Ted Drake. That season culminated with Arsenal winning the league championship for the first time in their history. He captured another league title in 1932/33, his last full season for the club. He moved on to Fulham and finished his career at Margate.

Lambert currently holds three Arsenal scoring records. Aside from sharing the record of most hat-tricks in a single season with Drake, his final tally of 12 hat-tricks for the club is a record he shares Jimmy Brain, and he is the only Arsenal player to have scored five goals in a single match at Highbury.

ARSENAL GOALS

Date	Opponents	Competition	Goals
16 October 1926	West Ham United	League	1
12 December 1927	Bury	League	1
18 February 1928	Aston Villa	FA Cup	1
07 March 1928	Liverpool	League	1
14 March 1928	Sunderland	League	1
29 September 1928	Huddersfield Town	League	1
14 September 1929	Burnley	League	2
21 September 1929	Sunderland	League	1
19 October 1929	Grimsby Town	League	3
11 January 1930	Chelsea	FA Cup	1
08 February 1930	Everton	League	3
15 February 1930	Middlesbrough	FA Cup	1
22 February 1930	Grimsby Town	League	1
01 March 1930	West Ham United	FA Cup	2
12 March 1930	Manchester United	League	1
29 March 1930	Blackburn Rovers	League	2
12 April 1930	Sheffield United	League	3
26 April 1930	Huddersfield Town	FA Cup	1
03 May 1930	Aston Villa	League	2
01 September 1930	Bolton Wanderers	League	3
06 September 1930	Leeds United	League	2
13 September 1930	Sunderland	League	3
15 September 1930	Blackburn Rovers	League	1
20 September 1930	Leicester City	League	2
27 September 1930	Birmingham City	League	3
04 October 1930	Sheffield United	League	1
18 October 1930	Manchester United	League	1
08 November 1930	Aston Villa	League	1
15 November 1930	Sheffield Wednesday	League	2
22 November 1930	Middlesbrough	League	3
29 November 1930	Chelsea	League	1
25 December 1930	Manchester City	League	1
10 January 1931	Aston Villa	FA Cup	1
28 January 1931	Grimsby Town	League	3
31 January 1931	Birmingham City	League	1

THE 100 CLUB

05 February 1931	Leicester City	League	3
28 March 1931	Middlesbrough	League	3
11 April 1931	Grimsby Town	League	1
18 April 1931	Liverpool	League	1
02 May 1931	Bolton Wanderers	League	2
05 September 1931	Birmingham City	League	1
09 September 1931	Portsmouth	League	2
19 September 1931	Manchester City	League	1
26 September 1931	Everton	League	1
03 October 1931	Grimsby Town	League	1
10 October 1931	Blackpool	League	1
07 November 1931	Newcastle United	League	1
28 November 1931	Liverpool	League	3
19 December 1931	Middlesbrough	League	1
09 January 1932	Darwen	FA Cup	2
23 January 1932	Plymouth Argyle	FA Cup	2
25 March 1932	Derby County	League	2
26 March 1932	West Ham United	League	1
02 April 1932	Chelsea	League	1
09 April 1932	Liverpool	League	1
27 April 1932	Huddersfield Town	League	1
30 April 1932	Middlesbrough	League	2
07 May 1932	Blackburn Rovers	League	2
05 November 1932	Wolves	League	2
19 November 1932	Aston Villa	League	1
24 December 1932	Sheffield United	League	5
07 January 1933	Sunderland	League	2
01 April 1933	Aston Villa	League	2
14 April 1933	Sheffield Wednesday	League	1
15 April 1933	Portsmouth	League	1
06 September 1933	West Bromwich Albion	League	1

FRANK STAPLETON

Arsenal Goals: 108
Arsenal Debut: *Arsenal v Stoke City, 23 March 1975*
First Arsenal Goal: *Arsenal v Leicester City, 6 September 1975*
Last Arsenal Goal: *Wolves v Arsenal, 25 April 1981*
Arsenal Honours: *FA Cup 1979*
Individual Honours: *None*
International Caps: *71 (20 goals, Republic Of Ireland)*

Frank Stapleton was one of the best in the business in his position. Tall and strong, he was deadly inside and outside the box and an excellent header of the ball. He joined Arsenal as an apprentice in 1972, making his debut in 1975, playing in three successive FA Cup finals for the Gunners from 1978 – 1980 and was a scorer in the 1979 win over Manchester United.

He moved to United in the summer of 1981, helping them to two FA Cups, in 1983 and 1985. In the first of these, Stapleton became the first player to score in FA Cup finals for two different clubs. He left United at the end of Alex Ferguson's first season in charge to join Ajax but made only six appearances before moving on to Anderlecht of Belgium. A loan move back to England with Derby County followed with stints at Le Havre in France and Blackburn Rovers before winding his career down at Aldershot, Huddersfield Town, Bradford City – where he was player-manager – and Brighton where he played only twice more before hanging his boots up.

ARSENAL GOALS

Date	Opponents	Competition	Goals
06 September 1975	Leicester City	League	1
09 September 1975	Everton	League Cup	1
20 September 1975	Everton	League	1
25 October 1975	Middlesbrough	League	1
17 April 1976	Ipswich Town	League	1
25 August 1976	Norwich City	League	1
11 September 1976	West Ham United	League	1
18 September 1976	Everton	League	1
02 October 1976	Queens Park Rangers	League	1
05 October 1976	Blackpool	League Cup	1
23 October 1976	Leicester City	League	1
26 October 1976	Chelsea	League Cup	1
06 November 1976	Birmingham City	League	1
27 November 1976	Coventry City	League	1
01 December 1976	Queens Park Rangers	League	1
04 December 1976	Newcastle United	League Cup	1
29 January 1977	Coventry City	FA Cup	1
19 February 1977	West Ham United	League	1
09 April 1977	West Bromwich Albion	League	1
23 April 1977	Coventry City	League	1
07 May 1977	Middlesbrough	League	1
14 May 1977	Manchester United	League	1
03 September 1977	Nottingham Forest	League	2
17 September 1977	Leicester City	League	1
01 October 1977	West Ham United	League	1
25 October 1977	Southampton	League Cup	1
05 November 1977	Manchester United	League	1
19 November 1977	Newcastle United	League	1
29 November 1977	Hull City	League Cup	1
17 December 1977	Coventry City	League	2
07 January 1978	Sheffield United	FA Cup	2
14 January 1978	Wolves	League	1
18 February 1978	Walsall	FA Cup	2
18 March 1978	Bristol City	League	2
22 April 1978	Leeds United	League	1

FRANK STAPLETON

29 April 1978	Middlesbrough	League	1
29 August 1978	Rotherham United	League Cup	1
02 September 1978	Queens Park Rangers	League	2
13 September 1978	Lokomotiv Leipzig	UEFA Cup	2
16 September 1978	Bolton Wanderers	League	1
27 September 1978	Lokomotiv Leipzig	UEFA Cup	2
28 October 1978	Bristol City	League	1
04 November 1978	Ipswich Town	League	3
25 November 1978	Coventry City	League	1
16 December 1978	Derby County	League	1
23 December 1978	Tottenham Hotspur	League	1
30 December 1978	Birmingham City	League	1
13 January 1979	Nottingham Forest	League	1
17 January 1979	Sheffield Wednesday	FA Cup	2
22 January 1979	Sheffield Wednesday	FA Cup	1
26 February1979	Nottingham Forest	FA Cup	1
10 March 1979	Bristol City	League	1
31 March 1979	Wolves	FA Cup	1
10 April 1979	Tottenham Hotspur	League	1
16 April 1979	Chelsea	League	2
25 April 1979	Aston Villa	League	1
12 May 1979	Manchester United	FA Cup	1
18 August 1979	Brighton	League	1
29 August 1979	Leeds United	League Cup	1
04 September 1979	Leeds United	League Cup	1
08 September 1979	Derby County	League	1
15 September 1979	Middlesbrough	League	1
25 September 1979	Southampton	League Cup	1
29 September 1979	Wolves	League	1
13 November 1979	Brighton	League Cup	2
17 November 1979	Everton	League	2
01 December 1979	Nottingham Forest	League	1
08 December 1979	Coventry City	League	1
15 December 1979	West Bromwich Albion	League	1
21 December 1979	Norwich City	League	1
16 February 1980	Bolton Wanderers	FA Cup	1
19 February 1980	Bolton Wanderers	FA Cup	1
23 February 1980	Bolton Wanderers	League	1
08 March 1980	Watford	FA Cup	2

15 March 1980	Manchester United	League	1
26 April 1980	West Bromwich Albion	League	1
16 May 1980	Wolves	League	1
16 August 1980	West Bromwich Albion	League	1
19 August 1980	Southampton	League	1
23 August 1980	Coventry City	League	1
26 August 1980	Swansea City	League Cup	1
30 August 1980	Tottenham Hotspur	League	1
22 September 1980	Stockport County	League Cup	1
04 October 1980	Leicester City	League	1
22 November 1980	Everton	League	1
06 December 1980	Wolves	League	1
26 December 1980	Crystal Palace	League	1
31 January 1981	Coventry City	League	1
07 February 1981	Stoke City	League	1
21 February 1981	Nottingham Forest	League	1
28 February 1981	Middlesbrough	League	1
31 March 1981	Birmingham City	League	1
25 April 1981	Wolves	League	1

THEO WALCOTT

Arsenal Goals: 108
Arsenal Debut: *Arsenal v Aston Villa, 19 August 2006*
First Arsenal Goal: *Arsenal v Chelsea, 25 February 2007*
Last Arsenal Goal: *Arsenal v Bate Borisov, 07 December 2017*
Arsenal Honours: *FA Cup 2015, 2017*
                     Charity / Community Shield 2015, 2017
Individual Honours: *None*
International Caps: *47 (8 goals, England)*

Theo Walcott's professional career began with Southampton, where he became their youngest ever player at 16 years and 143 days, and he soon became their youngest ever goal scorer.

He was signed by Arsène Wenger in January 2006, making his debut on the opening day of the 2006/07 season. He scored his first Arsenal goal in the League Cup final in February 2007, although the Gunners were beaten 2-1 by Chelsea that day.

Walcott became a regular in Arsenal's first team in the 2008/09 season but, frustratingly, saw his Arsenal career punctuated by a series of injuries. When he was fit and playing, though, Walcott's tremendous pace made him a frightening prospect for any defence to face.

He gained two FA Cup winners medals with the Gunners, scoring the opening goal in the 2015 final against Aston Villa in a game Arsenal went on to win 4-0. His second medal came two seasons later in a 2-1 win over Chelsea.

Such was Walcott's impact when he burst onto the scene as a youngster that he was chosen by England manager Sven-Göran Eriksson for the 2006 World Cup before he had even played a senior game for Arsenal following his transfer from Southampton, although he wasn't used during the tournament. In the lead-up to the competition, Walcott became England's youngest senior international, a record he still holds to this day.

Walcott left Arsenal in January 2018 to join Everton and returned to fist club Southampton, firstly on loan, and then permanently in 2020.

ARSENAL GOALS

Date	Opponents	Competition	Goals
25 February 2007	Chelsea	League Cup	1
23 October 2007	Slavia Prague	Champions League	2
09 January 2008	Tottenham Hotspur	League Cup	1
23 February 2008	Birmingham City	League	2
28 April 2008	Derby County	League	1
11 May 2008	Sunderland	League	1
27 August 2008	FC Twente	Champions League	1
18 October 2008	Everton	League	1
21 October 2008	Fenerbahce	Champions League	1
11 April 2009	Wigan Athletic	League	1
15 April 2009	Villarreal	Champions League	1
18 April 2009	Chelsea	FA Cup	1
04 October 2009	Blackburn Rovers	League	1
06 March 2010	Burnley	League	1
31 March 2010	Barcelona	Champions League	1
18 April 2010	Wigan Athletic	League	1
21 August 2010	Blackpool	League	3
28 August 2010	Blackburn Rovers	League	1
27 October 2010	Newcastle United	League Cup	2
03 November 2010	Shakhtar Donetsk	Champions League	1
08 December 2010	Partizan Belgrade	Champions League	1
27 December 2010	Chelsea	League	1
15 January 2011	West Ham United	League	1
05 February 2011	Newcastle United	League	1
20 April 2011	Tottenham Hotspur	League	1
22 May 2011	Fulham	League	1
16 August 2011	Udinese	Champions League	1
24 August 2011	Udinese	Champions League	1
28 August 2011	Manchester United	League	1
29 October 2011	Chelsea	League	1
15 January 2012	Swansea City	League	1
29 January 2012	Aston Villa	FA Cup	1
26 February 2012	Tottenham Hotspur	League	2
24 March 2012	Aston Villa	League	1
31 March 2012	Queens Park Rangers	League	1

THE 100 CLUB

11 April 2012	Wolves	League	1
15 September 2012	Southampton	League	1
26 September 2012	Coventry City	League Cup	2
06 October 2012	West Ham United	League	1
30 October 2012	Reading	League Cup	3
06 November 2012	Schalke	Champions League	1
17 November 2012	Tottenham Hotspur	League	1
28 November 2012	Everton	League	1
17 December 2012	Reading	League	1
29 December 2012	Newcastle United	League	3
20 January 2013	Chelsea	League	1
23 January 2013	West Ham United	League	1
26 January 2013	Brighton	FA Cup	1
30 January 2013	Liverpool	League	1
28 April 2013	Manchester United	League	1
04 May 2013	Queens Park Rangers	League	1
14 May 2013	Wigan Athletic	League	1
18 September 2013	Marseille	Champions League	1
14 December 2013	Manchester City	League	2
26 December 2013	West Ham United	League	2
01 January 2014	Cardiff City	League	1
25 January 2015	Brighton	FA Cup	1
01 February 2015	Aston Villa	League	1
10 February 2015	Leicester City	League	1
24 May 2015	West Bromwich Albion	League	3
30 May 2015	Aston Villa	FA Cup	1
12 September 2015	Stoke City	League	1
16 September 2015	Dinamo Zagreb	Champions League	1
26 September 2015	Leicester City	League	1
29 September 2015	Olympiakos	Champions League	1
21 December 2015	Manchester City	League	1
14 February 2016	Leicester City	League	1
08 March 2016	Hull City	FA Cup	2
02 April 2016	Watford	League	1
14 August 2016	Liverpool	League	1
17 September 2016	Hull City	League	1
24 September 2016	Chelsea	League	1
28 September 2016	Basel	Champions League	2
15 October 2016	Swansea City	League	2

THEO WALCOTT

19 October 2016	Ludogorets	Champions League	1
27 November 2016	Bournemouth	League	1
10 December 2016	Stoke City	League	1
18 December 2016	Manchester City	League	1
28 January 2017	Southampton	FA Cup	3
20 February 2017	Sutton United	FA Cup	1
07 March 2017	Bayern Munich	Champions League	1
11 March 2017	Lincoln City	FA Cup	1
02 April 2017	Manchester City	League	1
05 April 2017	West Ham United	League	1
20 September 2017	Doncaster Rovers	League Cup	1
28 September 2017	Bate Borisov	Europa League	2
07 December 2017	Bate Borisov	Europa League	1

DAVID HERD

Arsenal Goals: 107
Arsenal Debut: Arsenal v Leicester City, 19 February 1955
First Arsenal Goal: Portsmouth v Arsenal, 30 April 1955
Last Arsenal Goal: Everton v Arsenal, 29 April 1961
Arsenal Honours: None
Individual Honours: None
International Caps: 5 (3 goals, Scotland)

David Herd was born in Lanarkshire in Scotland but grew up in Manchester due to his father Alex playing for Manchester City and later Stockport County, and it was with Stockport that Herd made his league debut. After only 15 games, he attracted the attention of Arsenal manager Tom Whittaker and made the move south in 1954.

His first couple of seasons at Highbury saw him mainly used as back-up, but his breakthrough came in the 1956/57 season when he scored 18 goals to establish himself in the starting line-up. He finished as top scorer for four seasons in a row although, unfortunately for Herd, his time with Arsenal coincided with a trophy drought, and he went unrewarded for his scoring exploits.

He joined Manchester United for the 1961/62 season, continuing where he left off at Arsenal by regularly hitting the back of the net. At United he won two league championships and scored two goals in the 1963 FA Cup final against Leicester, United winning the game 3-1. He was part of the United squad that won the European Cup in 1968, although he took no part in the final. After his time in Manchester, he had stints with Stoke City and Waterford United before hanging up his boots.

ARSENAL GOALS

Date	Opponents	Competition	Goals
30 April 1955	Portsmouth	League	1
04 February 1956	Sunderland	League	2
20 October 1956	Tottenham Hotspur	League	2
15 December 1956	Cardiff City	League	2
05 January 1957	Stoke City	FA Cup	2
12 January 1957	Portsmouth	League	1
26 January 1957	Newport County	FA Cup	1
02 February 1957	Sheffield Wednesday	League	3
09 February 1957	Manchester United	League	2
16 February 1957	Preston North End	FA Cup	1
19 February 1957	Preston North End	FA Cup	1
02 Match 1957	West Bromwich Albion	FA Cup	1
06 April 1957	Leeds United	League	1
22 April 1957	Blackpool	League	1
27 August 1957	West Bromwich Albion	League	2
14 September 1957	Leicester City	League	1
21 September 1957	Manchester United	League	1
28 September 1957	Leeds United	League	2
02 October 1957	Aston Villa	League	1
05 October 1957	Bolton Wanderers	League	1
16 October 1957	Everton	League	1
16 November 1957	Portsmouth	League	2
14 December 1957	Preston North End	League	1
21 December 1957	Sunderland	League	2
11 January 1958	Blackpool	League	2
01 February 1958	Manchester United	League	1
22 February 1958	Tottenham Hotspur	League	1
08 March 1958	Chelsea	League	3
15 March 1958	Manchester City	League	1
22 March 1958	Sheffield Wednesday	League	1
12 April 1958	Newcastle United	League	1
06 September 1958	Everton	League	4
09 September 1958	Bolton Wanderers	League	1
13 September 1958	Tottenham Hotspur	League	2
20 September 1958	Manchester City	League	2

27 September 1958	Leeds United	League	1
04 October 1958	West Bromwich Albion	League	1
15 November 1958	Nottingham Forest	League	1
10 January 1959	Bury	FA Cup	1
28 January 1959	Colchester United	FA Cup	2
24 February 1959	Leeds United	League	1
31 January 1959	Tottenham Hotspur	League	1
28 February 1959	Manchester United	League	1
29 August 1959	Wolves	League	2
01 September 1959	Nottingham Forest	League	1
09 September 1959	Bolton Wanderers	League	1
15 September 1959	Bolton Wanderers	League	1
19 September 1959	Blackburn Rovers	League	1
26 September 1959	Blackpool	League	1
10 October 1959	Manchester United	League	1
31 October 1959	Birmingham City	League	1
07 November 1959	Leeds United	League	1
06 February 1960	Blackburn Rovers	League	1
15 March 1960	Leicester City	League	1
26 March 1960	Leeds United	League	1
15 April 1960	Fulham	League	1
20 August 1960	Burnley	League	1
06 September 1960	Birmingham City	League	1
10 September 1960	Tottenham Hotspur	League	1
17 September 1960	Newcastle United	League	3
01 October 1960	West Bromwich Albion	League	1
15 October 1960	Aston Villa	League	1
22 October 1960	Blackburn Rovers	League	1
29 October 1960	Manchester United	League	1
19 November 1960	Blackpool	League	1
26 November 1960	Everton	League	3
03 December 1960	Wolves	League	2
17 December 1960	Burnley	League	1
31 December 1960	Nottingham Forest	League	3
07 January 1961	Sunderland	FA Cup	1
14 January 1961	Manchester City	League	3
11 February 1961	Cardiff City	League	2
31 March 1961	Fulham	League	2
08 April 1961	Blackpool	League	1
29 April 1961	Everton	League	1

OLIVIER GIROUD

Arsenal Goals: 105
Arsenal Debut: Arsenal v Sunderland, 18 August 2012
First Arsenal Goal: Arsenal v Coventry City, 26 September 2012
Last Arsenal Goal: Southampton v Arsenal, 10 December 2017
Arsenal Honours: FA Cup 2014, 2015, 2017
Charity / Community Shield 2014, 2015, 2017
Individual Honours: FIFA Puskas Award 2017
Knight Of The Legion Of Honour 2018
International Caps: 110 (46 goals, France)

Olivier Giroud began his career in France with Grenoble, before moving on to Tours and Montpellier, with whom he won the first league championship in the club's history. His exploits in the French league won him a transfer to Arsenal in 2012.

The following season, 2013/14, saw Giroud's goals helped Arsenal to the FA Cup. He scored twice in the quarter-final and also one of the penalties in the semi-final shoot-out. In the final itself, he set up the winning goal for Aaron Ramsey as Arsenal beat Hull City 3-2, coming back from two goals down.

The Gunners retained the trophy in 2015 thanks to a 4-0 win over Aston Villa. Giroud started the game amongst the substitutes but climbed off the bench to claim the fourth Arsenal goal.

Perhaps Giroud's greatest individual moment came in a Premier League game against Crystal Palace in the 2016/17 season when he scored with a 'scorpion kick' that Arsène Wenger described as the best goal he had ever seen at the Emirates Stadium. He arrived just too early to connect with a cross but back heeled the ball over his head and into the net. The goal won him the 2017 Puskas Award, a trophy given to the player who has scored the most beautiful goal in world football that calendar year.

Giroud joined Chelsea in January 2018 in a transfer triangle that saw him replace Michy Batshuayi at Stamford Bridge after he left for Borussia Dortmund to replace Pierre-Emerick Aubameyang who moved to Arsenal. At Chelsea, Giroud won his fourth FA Cup and helped his new team beat his old Arsenal team mates in the UEFA League final in 2019. He left Stamford Bridge to join AC Milan for the 2021/22 season.

Aside from his glittering club career, Giroud is also an international champion, being part of the French squad that won the World Cup in 2018.

ARSENAL GOALS

Date	Opponents	Competition	Goals
26 September 2012	Coventry City	League Cup	1
06 October 2012	West Ham United	League	1
30 October 2012	Reading	League Cup	1
06 November 2012	Schalke	Champions League	1
10 November 2012	Fulham	League	2
17 November 2012	Tottenham Hotspur	League	1
29 December 2012	Newcastle United	League	2
23 January 2013	West Ham United	League	2
26 January 2013	Brighton	FA Cup	2
30 January 2013	Liverpool	League	1
13 March 2013	Bayern Munich	Champions League	1
30 March 2013	Reading	League	1
13 April 2013	Norwich City	League	1
17 August 2013	Aston Villa	League	1
21 August 2013	Fenerbahce	Champions League	1
24 August 2013	Fulham	League	1
01 September 2013	Tottenham Hotspur	League	1
14 September 2013	Sunderland	League	1
01 October 2013	Napoli	Champions League	1
22 October 2013	Borussia Dortmund	Champions League	1
26 October 2013	Crystal Palace	League	1
23 November 2013	Southampton	League	2
29 December 2013	Newcastle United	League	1
13 January 2014	Aston Villa	League	1
24 January 2014	Coventry City	FA Cup	1
28 January 2014	Southampton	League	1
22 February 2014	Sunderland	League	2
08 March 2014	Everton	FA Cup	2
25 March 2014	Swansea City	League	1
15 April 2014	West Ham United	League	1
28 April 2014	Newcastle United	League	1
04 May 2014	West Bromwich Albion	League	1
10 August 2014	Manchester City	Community Shield	1
23 August 2014	Everton	League	1
22 November 2014	Manchester United	League	1

13 December 2014	Newcastle United	League	2
21 December 2014	Liverpool	League	1
18 January 2015	Manchester City	League	1
01 February 2015	Aston Villa	League	1
15 February 2015	Middlesbrough	FA Cup	2
21 February 2015	Crystal Palace	League	1
01 March 2015	Everton	League	1
04 March 2015	Queens Park Rangers	League	1
14 March 2015	West Ham United	League	1
17 March 2015	Monaco	Champions League	1
21 March 2015	Newcastle United	League	2
04 April 2015	Liverpool	League	1
30 May 2015	Aston Villa	FA Cup	1
16 August 2015	Crystal Palace	League	1
12 September 2015	Stoke City	League	1
26 September 2015	Leicester City	League	1
17 October 2015	Watford	League	1
20 October 2015	Bayern Munich	Champions League	1
24 October 2015	Everton	League	1
31 October 2015	Swansea	League	1
04 November 2015	Bayern Munich	Champions League	1
21 November 2015	West Bromwich Albion	League	1
05 December 2015	Sunderland	League	1
09 December 2015	Olympiakos	Champions League	3
13 December 2015	Aston Villa	League	1
21 December 2015	Manchester City	League	1
09 January 2016	Sunderland	FA Cup	1
13 January 2016	Liverpool	League	2
08 March 2016	Hull City	FA Cup	2
08 May 2016	Manchester City	League	1
15 May 2016	Aston Villa	League	3
29 October 2016	Sunderland	League	2
01 November 2016	Ludogorets	Champions League	1
19 November 2016	Manchester United	League	1
23 November 2016	Paris St Germain	Champions League	1
26 December 2016	West Bromwich Albion	League	1
01 January 2017	Crystal Palace	League	1
03 January 2017	Bournemouth	League	1
07 January 2017	Preston North End	FA Cup	1

OLIVIER GIROUD

14 January 2017	Swansea City	League	1
04 February 2017	Chelsea	League	1
11 March 2017	Lincoln City	FA Cup	1
05 April 2017	West Ham United	League	1
10 May 2017	Southampton	League	1
13 May 2017	Stoke City	League	2
11 August 2017	Leicester City	League	1
28 September 2017	Bate Borisov	Europa League	1
19 October 2017	Red Star Belgrade	Europa League	1
29 November 2017	Huddersfield Town	League	2
07 December 2017	Bate Borisov	Europa League	1
10 December 2017	Southampton	League	1

JOE BAKER

Arsenal Goals:	*100*
Arsenal Debut:	*Leyton Orient v Arsenal, 18 August 1962*
First Arsenal Goal:	*Leyton Orient v Arsenal, 18 August 1962*
Last Arsenal Goal:	*Arsenal v Sheffield Wednesday, 28 December 1965*
Arsenal Honours:	*None*
Individual Honours:	*None*
International Caps:	*8 (3 goals, England)*

Joe Baker was born in Liverpool but grew up in Scotland where he began his football career playing for Hibernian. His scoring record was prolific, including an astonishing nine goals in one Scottish Cup tie against Peebles Rovers. He left for Torino, where he played the 1961/62 season alongside Denis Law who also joined that summer. Unfortunately for Baker, his time in Italy almost ended tragically when he needed life saving surgery after a car crash.

Having recovered from his injuries, Baker joined Arsenal in time for the 1962/63 season for a then club record fee of £70,000. He scored on his debut against Orient and, for three of his four seasons at Highbury, finished as the club's top scorer. His 100th and last Arsenal goal came against Sheffield Wednesday in December 1965.

After moving away from Highbury, Baker joined Nottingham Forest before moving to Sunderland and then back up to Scotland for his second spell at Hibernian and then, lastly, Raith Rovers.

Baker was the first player to have represented the England national team without having first played in the English league, having won his first international cap during his time with Hibernian.

ARSENAL GOALS

Date	Opponents	Competition	Goals
18 August 1962	Leyton Orient	League	1
21 August 1962	Birmingham City	League	1
08 September 1962	Sheffield Wednesday	League	1
10 September 1962	Aston Villa	League	1
15 September 1962	Fulham	League	1
22 September 1962	Leicester City	League	1
13 October 1962	West Ham United	League	1
27 October 1962	Wolves	League	3
03 November 1962	Blackburn Rovers	League	2
24 November 1962	Ipswich Town	League	1
01 December 1962	Manchester City	League	1
15 December 1962	Leyton Orient	League	2
30 January 1963	Oxford United	FA Cup	2
23 February 1963	Tottenham Hotspur	League	1
02 March 1963	West Ham United	League	2
26 March 1963	Everton	League	1
13 April 1963	Sheffield United	League	1
15 April 1963	West Bromwich Albion	League	2
06 May 1963	Manchester United	League	1
11 May 1963	Burnley	League	1
14 May 1963	Fulham	League	3
18 May 1963	Sheffield Wednesday	League	1
27 August 1963	West Bromwich Albion	League	2
07 September 1963	Bolton Wanderers	League	1
09 September 1963	Aston Villa	League	3
14 September 1963	Fulham	League	1
21 September 1963	Manchester United	League	1
25 September 1963	Staevnet	Fairs Cup	3
05 October 1963	Ipswich Town	League	2
09 October 1963	Stoke City	League	2
15 October 1963	Tottenham Hotspur	League	1
02 November 196	Sheffield United	League	1
05 November 1963	Birmingham City	League	3
30 November 1963	Blackburn Rovers	League	1
07 December 1963	Liverpool	League	1

10 December 1963	Everton	League	2
28 December 1963	Birmingham City	League	1
04 January 1964	Wolves	FA Cup	1
11 January 1964	Fulham	League	1
18 January 1964	Bolton Wanderers	League	1
25 January 1964	West Bromwich Albion	FA Cup	1
29 February 1964	Stoke City	League	1
14 March 1964	Chelsea	League	1
22 August 1964	Liverpool	League	1
02 September 1964	Sheffield Wednesday	League	1
08 September 1964	Blackburn Rovers	League	1
16 September 1964	Blackburn Rovers	League	1
19 September 1964	Leicester City	League	1
10 October 1964	Tottenham Hotspur	League	1
17 October 1964	Burnley	League	1
31 October 1964	Everton	League	2
07 November 1964	Birmingham City	League	1
05 December 1964	Fulham	League	2
19 December 1964	Aston Villa	League	1
26 December 1964	Stoke City	League	1
02 January 1965	Wolves	League	1
16 January 1965	Sunderland	League	1
23 January 1965	Leicester City	League	2
20 February 1965	Fulham	League	1
23 February 1965	Tottenham Hotspur	League	2
27 March 1965	West Ham United	League	1
06 April 1965	Birmingham City	League	1
19 April 1965	Blackpool	League	2
21 August 1965	Stoke City	League	2
28 August 1965	Burnley	League	1
04 September 1965	Chelsea	League	1
11 September 1965	Tottenham Hotspur	League	1
18 September 1965	Everton	League	1
25 September 1965	Manchester United	League	1
09 October 1965	Fulham	League	1
23 October 1965	Blackburn Rovers	League	1
06 November 1965	Sheffield United	League	2
20 November 1965	West Ham United	League	1
28 December 1965	Sheffield Wednesday	League	1

ACKNOWLEDGMENTS

There are a few people without whom this book may never have come about.

Firstly, my wife Melanie must receive many thanks for her support during this project for many things, not least for keeping the cupboards stocked with coffee and biscuits to aid me in my venture.

Then, of course, there are the 19 players who have scored 100 goals or more for Arsenal Football Club. Needless to say, without you there would be no book.

Special thanks must also go to Alan Smith. Not only a member of the 100 Club but also for agreeing to write the foreword. I don't know how high this will rank in his career highlights alongside league championships, England appearances and scoring the winner in the final of the European Cup Winners' Cup, but for me it is right up there.

Plus, of course, thanks to my publishers Morgan Lawrence for the help they have given and trust they have shown.

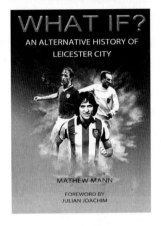
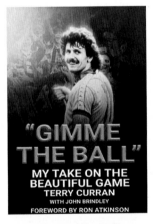
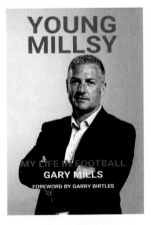

MORGAN LAWRENCE
P U B L I S H I N G   S E R V I C E S

The following books are also available to purchase from morganlawrence.co.uk and all major book retailers

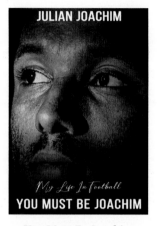

You Must Be Joachim

By Julian Joachim

The Reality of the Dream

By Malcolm Christie

Coming soon

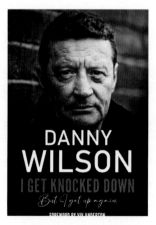

I Get Knocked Down

By Danny Wilson

Email: hello@morganlawrence.co.uk
Telephone: 07514 116 493